MW00987408

When RELIGION is an ADDICTION

Robert N. Minor, Ph.D.

HumanityWorks!
A CONSORTIUM BUILDING:

Connection
Community
Cooperation
Collaboration

Published by HumanityWorks!
4047 Botanical Avenue, Suite 200
St. Louis, MO 63110-3905

Publisher's Cataloging-in-Publication
(Provided by Quality Books, Inc.)

    Minor, Robert Neil, 1945-
      When religion is an addiction / Robert N. Minor.
      p. cm.
      Includes bibliographical references.
      LCCN: 2007931508
      ISBN-13: 978-0-9709581-2-9
      ISBN-10: 0-9709581-2-9

      1. Religious addiction–Christianity. 2. Influence (Psychology)–Religious aspects. 3. Christianity and culture–United States. 4. God (Christianity)–Knowableness. I. Title.

BR114.M56 2007   261
                  QBI07-1627

Cover design and book layout by The Rockhold Group.

CONTENTS

INTRODUCTION

You'd have to be living on another planet in a galaxy far, far away to miss the influence of the religious, specifically Christian, right-wing in the US today. They've made themselves difficult to ignore.

In fact, like the most dysfunctional person in a typical, traditional family, the religious right-wing has become the center of the country's attention politically, religiously, and socially. Like the family drunk, they are on a bender and their current drink is political. Election days for them have begun to look like New Years' Eve for an alcoholic.

They're setting the agenda to which other political, religious, and activist groups are having to respond. And the responses have more often been like those of an addict's enablers.

The religious right-wing now provides a target constituency for votes and funds for the Republican Party, and even some Democrats. It successfully seated a president whom its members continue to insist is "a fine Christian man" no matter what he does. It's become an intimate partner with US consumerism and "free market" big-business economic interests no matter how poor the first-century followers of its Jesus were.

What media analyst David Brock calls *The Republican Noise Machine* with its right-wing Christian radio and TV stations, and a right-wing corporate media symbolized by the FOX News cable network, support this right-wing Christianity. On top of all that, the mainstream media feel they must continue to provide the religious right-wing with attention and a legitimacy far beyond the numbers it represents. They've become a crucial part of the right-wing's family of enablers.

The mainstream media often seek out right-wing religion

to provide *the* balance to other viewpoints that aren't even about religion at all. A 2007 study by the watchdog group Media Matters of America finds that on the three major television networks, the three major cable news channels, and PBS, right-wing religious leaders were interviewed, quoted, or mentioned almost 3.8 times as often as other religious leaders on all issues.

The media thereby define the debate in almost all national discussions as the religious right-wing on one side and the other side occupied by science, social science, academics, or anything and anyone else. It's as if, for example, debates over stem-cell research pit science against morality with only a right-wing Christian religio-political version of morality posed as the "other side." It's as if the only alternatives in discussions of evolution are right-wing Christian creationism or atheism.

Right-wing religion fomented "Culture Wars" in the US that enable it to continue to set a warrior-style political strategy regarding what we've come to call "social issues," while it acts as if making war on other people and nations isn't a social or "values" issue at all. It's so driving the national agenda that most of the country is caught up in its religiously motivated political and social initiatives.

Outsiders express amazement when they hear right-wing religious leaders, ministers, televangelists, and their political bedfellows speak, or when they learn about their latest political initiative to force US citizens to act more like its version of what a Christian is. They're astonished by the right-wing's rewriting of history, callousness toward the beliefs, feelings, hurts, and deaths of others, the right-wing's moral inconsistencies and hypocrisies, and inability to listen seriously to the multitude of other viewpoints that US citizens hold.

Outsiders aren't surprised at all that right-wing people disagree with them. By now they expect that.

What really amazes them is the psychology of members of the religious right-wing, their attitudes and manner. Those outside the right-wing are struck by the fervency, obsessive busyness, closed-mindedness, and divisive energy that drive the religious right-wing. They're shocked by the right-wing's dogmatic assertion of its cause as uniquely just and righteous while painting those who disagree as mortal enemies out to destroy the family, God, humanity, the nation, faith, and civilization itself.

On the one hand, it was at first often difficult for outsiders to take the religious right-wing seriously. It's been hard for outsiders to believe that anyone could really believe all of this. It was easy to write the religious right-wing off as a group of nutcases.

So liberals turned to the usual inoffensive liberal responses to try to understand these right-wing people and to help the right-wing "see" and "understand" what they're doing and who they're hurting. Listen to what liberals find themselves saying:

"Lets' just sit down and dialogue with them as ladies and gentlemen. Then they'll stop this fevered push to remake the nation in their eyes and we'll all be able to work together."

"Let's just educate them with more facts. Then they'll see that what they're pushing for isn't rational and they'll become more open to the value of other people's concerns."

"Let's just seek compromises with them by giving them the benefit of the doubt, and moving our expectations closer to theirs. Then they'll surely be willing to compromise their goals, methods, and perspectives so as to embrace us too."

On the other hand, though, outsiders have been forced to take the religio-political right-wing seriously because it has changed the face of the country. Its juggernaut has so overwhelmed the political process that a few have even come to realize painfully that the old tactics of nice liberals don't work.

It's true that there are many people who reside in a moveable religious and political middle in the US. The 2006 Pew Research Center's report on religion and public life found that 49 percent believe Christian conservatives have gone too far "in trying to impose their religious values on the country."

For this middle, information and facts provide a basis for rethinking their faith and politics. For them, the usual nice, open-minded attempt to promote understanding is effective.

These are the people who can be reached if they're convinced: (1) that there really are viable alternatives to the religious right-wing and, most importantly, (2) that the people who hold these alternatives seriously, sincerely, and passionately bet their lives on these alternatives. They're not just doing political maneuvering to win elections.

I work regularly with members of this moveable middle right in the center of the country. They know something is wacky about what they're hearing from the religious-political right-wing. Many of them are still waiting for someone to speak with them who appears to sincerely and fervently hold a convincing alternative to what they hear constantly from mainstream and conservative media and even their own ministers.

But there are others for whom the facts are so trumped by the right-wing religious frame of reference they rely upon that they seem incapable of considering alternative views. Even harder would be real compromise or actual movement toward the proverbial political center. This group often includes religious personalities who have their careers, fame, finances, self-images, and ability to get attention and followers dependent upon their right-wing beliefs and practices.

This group also includes everyday followers who have become desperately dependent upon right-wing religious beliefs, practices, institutions, and leaders to alter their mood, to give them good feelings in the middle of a world that doesn't seem to care about them and their fortunes. These everyday folk cling desperately to these mood-altering substances for hope in a world that can scare them.

This book is about this latter group. It has the audacity to argue that for them religion is functioning as an addiction and that unless we understand that function and respond with it in mind, we'll be unable to affect the larger moveable middle in the long term.

Religion for this influential group is like a mood-altering substance upon which they've become increasingly dependent. In the last thirty years the addiction has encouraged them to seek stronger fixes. It has led them to become dependent upon the use of political activities and the elevated mood of political victories to alter their feelings about themselves.

In 1991 Father Leo Booth wrote a ground-breaking book on religious addiction: *When God Becomes a Drug: Breaking the Chains of Religious Abuse and Addiction*. Addiction expert, author, and counselor John Bradshaw, who in 1985 had recorded a set of cassettes entitled "Religious Addiction," wrote the book's foreword.

Booth's and Bradshaw's works were courageous. They took on an American icon. They broke with that old advice to never get into discussions about religion and politics. Out of their own experiences and their work with addicts, they spoke about the connection of religion and addiction in the same breath.

Over fifteen years later, their observations are still valuable, and in the meantime the addiction that uses religion has also become a dominant social and political force. We now must disregard that old advice again and speak plainly about both politics and religion.

Addictive religion has not only moved successfully into the political arena, but into the center of attention in the US in the same way that addicts usually become the center of attention in their families. From a marginal force in twentieth-century American society, addictive religion has set the nation's religious and political agenda.

Those outside the addiction have awakened to their own marginalization by the activities of these addicts. They've most often moved into a reactive mode toward the addicted that hasn't always been helpful.

Frankly, this movement of addictive religion could only have taken place because those of us outside religious addiction have enabled it to happen. Often we've done the best we knew how to do given our understanding of religion and our assumptions about how right-wing religion was functioning in people's lives.

Through minimizing the potential power of the religious right-wing, denial, obsessive positive or negative emotional attachment to it, and even self-blaming, we often became like abused spouses believing that there must be something we could do to control, change, or save the addicts. Our focus became changing them. That, we believed, would solve our problems.

This book is written as a result of my experience that one of the most requested topics in my speaking and workshops in the last few years is how to deal with religious people when you've tried everything else and nothing is working. Frustration among people who must respond to right-wing religion continues to build.

There's much anger, hurt, fretting, and hopelessness. People are getting tired, seeing it take a toll on their health, and realizing that their old responses are not only not changing much of the extreme religious right but encouraging it. They are also realizing that the religious right-wing's continual dominance of the discussion is hardly being affected by our current techniques.

When Religion is an Addiction first asks us to change our understanding of the radical religious right, to consider it in a new light, so that we can do something that will, first, ensure the health of those outside the addiction, and second, end our own activities that are part of the dynamics that further the religious right-wing. Chapters two through seven set out this new understanding and how it explains what we've been seeing happen around us.

Yet my ultimate goal is not only to set forth a way to understand the problem but also to point to solutions. Chapter one sets the tone for that at the beginning by calling us to stop arguing about religion in general. The recent spate of books that defend atheism — what *Time* magazine labelled "an atheist literary wave" — provides a welcome alternative voice in America's diverse religious dialogue. They encourage such arguments while they soothe the atheist choir.

Yet they actually provide more opportunities for the right-wing to further use religion as an addiction. They enable it to feel even more righteous and thereby not deal with the real issues that motivate its behavior.

Chapter eight discusses practical guidelines for dealing with people who use religion as their addiction. People in my workshops have already found these guidelines helpful, reassuring, and empowering.

However, I believe it's important for people to work out the application of those guidelines themselves. The process that groups go through of deciding how to respond to a specific addict without enabling is an important one for the group itself and is very situationally specific. How one responds to religious addicts and their political bedfellows in specific situations must be worked out on the ground.

Though the benefit of an outside perspective is often helpful, an outside consultant can only be a facilitator for what will become an important group experience. Creative and out-of-the-norm thinking by the group is important here.

In addition, we must recognize that appropriate, non-enabling responses will often not be the easiest to implement. But when we recognize the reality of the addiction, we'll see why we really have little choice.

When Religion is an Addiction isn't written for those who fit its description of religious addicts. For those for whom the shoe fits, I expect it will make them angry, more defensive, and even more reliant on claims that addicts make about how they are the real victims of everyone else. I expect them also to find relief in that defensiveness, in attacking the messenger, and in even more of their mood-altering addiction.

This is not because I am taking the view that addictions are rooted in moral problems. Right-wing religion itself has a history of viewing alcoholism and drug addiction as sinful. I instead join those addiction specialists who see the core of addictions, including religious addiction, as something more like a complex emotional disorder.

Addictions usually result in destructive and unethical behavior, but even that doesn't mean that the addict is some-how evil in some inherent way. These resulting behaviors, as addiction specialist Elizabeth Connell Henderson argues in *Understanding Addiction*, mean that no matter whether one sees addiction as a brain disorder, a disorder of the will, or a disease, it "can't be separated from morality and personal responsibility." "You may not have asked for the addiction," she writes, "but you must ask for help to recover, and you must be willing to accept responsibility for your choices."

Since completing this manuscript, former Nixon White House counsel and Barry Goldwater conservative, John W. Dean, has published his most important book to date. In *Conservatives Without Conscience* he brings to public atten-tion the sixty years of solid scientific research by behavioral scholars regarding what has been called "authoritarian per-sonalities."

This research shows that there is a large group of people in this country (possibly 20 percent or more of the populace) who are most comfortable living in submission to an authori-tarian figure or adopting the conscience of an authoritarian figure. With fear their underlying motivating factor, they feel safest when they set aside what would otherwise be their own moral views and shift consideration to how well they are liv-ing up to the expectations of an authority or authority figure. They are capable of doing great harm to others if they believe it to be sanctioned by the authority.

Because the results of these studies are so unusually and overwhelmingly conclusive for careful scientific research, it would be easy to make such solid scholarship seem less than the careful, controlled work it is. Dean has fortunately taken pains not to do so. That makes his thoughtful summary in dialogue with the researchers themselves an important addition to the understanding that informs my own work.

The research on authoritarianism shows overwhelmingly that this authoritarian stance is consistently associated with right-wing, but not left-wing, ideology. Dean quotes University of Manitoba Professor Robert Altemeyer, whose works include, *Right-Wing Authoritarianism* (1981), *Enemies of Freedom* (1988), *The Authoritarian Specter* (1996), and numerous peer-reviewed articles: "Now it turns out that in North America persons who score highly on my measure of authoritarianism test tend to favor right-wing political parties and have 'conservative' economic philosophies and religious sentiments."

The concept of addiction as the way religion is functioning for many people who include those Dean is describing, provides what Dean's work doesn't. It enforces our understanding of why people abandon their own moral values and accept the perspectives of those who deal in the addictive substance.

The addiction model also allows us to see what must be done to change this dynamic, rather than further it. It provides a model for responding effectively to our experiences with right-wing religious people and their abusive activities, especially if they fit these models of authoritarian personalities. As the country continues to be threatened by this addiction, there is hope to change things — if we have the courage to do so.

When Religion is an Addiction is written for those of us who are outside this addiction but can easily, by our very attempts to help, control, argue with, or change the addicts, fall into promoting the addiction instead. It's written with the primary goal of encouraging those outside the addiction to take a healthy stand for their own lives and for the lives of those around them.

It uses the insights of experts on religion, addiction, and addiction recovery. It's not, however, meant to defend or authoritatively represent any of the recovery methods, whether they are the programs of Alcoholics Anonymous, Narcotics Anonymous, Rational Recovery, or even Al-Anon.

No intervention in addiction has been 100% effective, whether it's these recovery programs, cognitive-behavioral therapy, motivational enhancement therapy, or relapse prevention therapy. Partly this might be because none of these methods touches upon a core piece of the problem people still must face when they emerge from treatments and group meetings — our society's current need for addictive behavior.

Yet, these programs offer great insight into addiction, addictive thinking, and dealing with addicts. They often provide a way to cut through the fog of addictive behavior and name it, its deceptive cover-ups, and its denial, for what they are.

I have not personally participated in any of these recovery programs. But in over the last twenty years I have paid attention, listened, researched, and learned from their experience and the words of recovering addicts. I've added their insights and experience to my own study of, and decades of experiences with, people all along the religious spectrum.

This book argues that we need a new way to frame and respond to right-wing religion as it functions for the many who dominate the religious-political scene today. It argues that we need a new response that's neither the old "nice" liberal one that's been tried again and again but has not worked well, nor the embittered anti-religion one that's contributing to the addiction.

It's written for non-religious, anti-religious, and religious people. And its immediate goal is to protect the health, sanity, and lives of the rest of us whose national and personal lives are heavily affected by religious believers when religion is an addiction.

CHAPTER ONE

RELIGION NEVER DOES ANYTHING

Isn't religion the cause of most wars?

Does praying make you a better person?

Why is religion so biased?

Doesn't religion make a nation more prosperous? More moral? More secure?

Don't empires and nations fall when they reject religion?

Is religion the same as spirituality?

People ask questions like these everyday, especially if they find out they're talking to a religious studies professor. Religion is a popular subject even though many of our parents used to warn us: "Never discuss religion or politics if you want to get along."

There are apparently enough people who'll give pat yes or no answers to these kinds of questions, too. So that seems to make us think that these types of questions are actually reasonably answerable.

However, the answers people give to these general questions about religion most often, and not surprisingly, arise more out of the respondents' own personal experiences with religious people, good or bad, than out of their own careful study of the historical evidence of the many religious and non-religious people around the world. Religion writers, parents, ministers, door-to-door religious salespeople, and televangelists have given most of us some deep-seated ideas about religion that are hard to shake, even when we'd rather ignore those messages.

"Hi," say the two sparkling, well-dressed people at the front door in the caption to an old cartoon. "We're here to read from the Bible and make you feel like dirt."

In many people's minds, religion deserves the blame for most of the world's problems, especially war and human suffering. They're convinced of this just as dogmatically as other people are convinced that religion (or *their* religion) provides the only real solution to those same problems.

There seems to be no end in sight to the on-going debates about religion in general — what it is, what it should be, what it means, whether it's good, bad, or neutral, whether it's too political, too public, really a private matter, and on and on. There's also no lack of opinions swirling all around the globe about what religion does or doesn't do.

One need not travel to India, as I did, to hear an educated businessman say: "All those holy men are just fakes. They're in it for the money and attention. That's what religion is about."

Many people feel they've been deeply hurt by the activities and attitudes, the judgments, demands and disappointments, the demeaning and finger-pointing, and the infighting and bitter debates that they've personally experienced in the religious groups with which they've come into contact. Many have never gotten over it either.

The coping mechanisms used by those who've been offended by painful experiences with religious people often include claiming that they're not "religious" at all. Maybe they tell us that they're not into something called "organized religion." They're into "spirituality," they say, or something else designated by a term that's somehow less offensive to them personally than whatever they call "religion."

Others whom we might identify as religious, claim that their religion is really not religion at all, but a faith, a tradition, a civilization, a way of life, or a personal relationship with the Divine. Clearly the word "religion" for many people has fallen on hard times. They'd prefer to think of religion as something other people do, believe, and practice, but not them.

Still others respond by rejecting all religion outright (including in their rejection of "religion" what others claim is really faith, tradition, a way of life, or a personal relationship to the Divine). Some people take every opportunity that comes their way to tell us they reject it. It's as if they can't let go of their past religious hurts, as if their deepest purpose in life has become personally seeing to the end of religion altogether.

The most extreme rejecters rail against religion the way some religious people rail against the heretics they want to root out of their own religion, the members of other religions, or the non-religious. They're convinced that the world would make progress without this thing called religion.

One writer in a 2005 issue of the *Journal of Religion and Society* has apparently concluded that we would be better off without religion. In an article with the hefty academic title "Cross-National Correlations of Quantifiable Societal Health with Popular Religiosity and Secularism in the Prosperous Democracies: A First Look," Baltimore researcher Gregory S. Paul compared data from 18 developed democracies.

He concluded: "In general, higher rates of belief in and worship of a creator correlate with higher rates of homicide, juvenile and early adult mortality, STD infection rates, teen pregnancy, and abortion.... None of the strongly secularized pro-evolution democracies is experiencing high levels of measurable dysfunction."

Other studies have shown a similar relationship between conservative religion and traditional measurements of lower morality within the US. A 1999 survey of the US conducted by the conservative Barna Research Group of Ventura, Calif., found that Baptists have the highest divorce rate of any Christian denomination and are more likely to get a divorce than atheists and agnostics.

Nationally, the states dubbed red by US media in recent presidential elections — Nevada, Tennessee, Arkansas, and Alabama — have the highest divorce rates in the country. It's none other than the very blue Massachusetts, which even values same-sex marriage, that has the lowest divorce rate.

It would be easy to conclude that religion is bad for us when we see such evidence pile up. The anti-religious will stand up and cheer. "See, we told you," they can remind us.

"REPENT! THE END OF RELIGION IS AT HAND"

In the last few centuries the number of predictions that religion is going to end became probably as large as the number of predictions that the Second Coming of Christ or the end of the world is at hand. What history has so far clearly shown is that both prophecies have exactly the same one hundred percent failure rate.

Whether it was the "Father of Sociology," Auguste Comte, or the "Father of Psychotherapy," Sigmund Freud, both looked forward to religion's end. Writers ever since have continued to hope, predict, and maybe secretly pray, that the end of religion was nigh.

Comte, the nineteenth century French positivist wrote that society goes through phases that began with the "Theological," where God is the reference for human activities, to the final phase, the "Scientific,' when people justify their actions as the will of the people alone. Freud, the turn of the century Austrian neurologist, was certain that the "illusion" of religion would be replaced by scientific answers and that religion would become obsolete.

Predictions of the triumph of secularism continue to this day, with a spectrum of religion's defenders arguing that the rise of secularism has impoverished the human condition. One hears much wishing and hoping on both sides with the prophets of religion's future demise or triumph continuing to preach their predictions to their respective, expectant choirs.

THERE IS NO RELIGION IN GENERAL

Blaming religion for societal and personal dysfunction is just as problematic as blaming the absence of religion for the same things. Accusing religion, or its absence, of causing a society's problems might make people feel better about whatever view of Reality they cling to, but either view gets us caught in a major error. The problem is that people are talking as if there were some actual entity in human experience called religion in general.

What's really going on is that when people want to pinpoint the effects of religion, they're not talking about some abstract entity in the heavens called religion but the religions they confront in the religious people they meet or read about every day. The history of "religion" is really many histories about people and groups with innumerable religious positions, beliefs, attitudes, actions, and practices.

General questions about what religion does or doesn't do, as well as the answers given to such questions, fail to make an important distinction that we, religious or not, will need to make in order to relate to religious people effectively and to understand how religions are functioning in people's lives to produce the variety of effects we observe, negative and positive.

Here then is where we begin to understand how religion functions in many people's lives the way addictions do. **There is no such thing as religion in general. All of us, in both the past and the present, experience religions only in the particular.**

Now, it's true that religious thinkers, theologians, and philosophers of both religion and irreligion have been writing for centuries about religion in general. Their discussions pour over the teachings, symbols, beliefs, and rituals of religions. They want to determine if they're true or false, good or evil, practical or impractical, and verifiable or fanciful. In the process of their thinking and writing about "religion," what they are actually doing is constructing their own personal ideal of a religion in general.

Other scholars, the historians and social scientists who observe religions on the ground, however, have questioned the whole idea of religion in general. For example, the acclaimed

historian of religions Wilfred Cantwell Smith in his 1964 classic, *The Meaning and End of Religion*, argued that we misun-
derstand religious people when we talk in terms of religion in
general.

If we really want to know about the religions of people as
people actually live them we must, Smith argued, begin with
the individual faiths of human beings. We must, he went so
far as to recommend, stop looking for religion or religions in
general.

Yet, in spite of such warnings, it seems that it's hard for
people to abandon thinking about religion in general. It's too
easy to fall back again and again into the error Smith pinpoint-
ed.

Publicly, there's certainly much talk about religion in general. It goes on and on. Writers still write about it, and people
still assume that there is an "it" to discuss.

But have you noticed that we never meet up with religion
in general? We've never experienced it. We've never found
some unembodied thing called religion so that we could say:
"Look there it goes, floating over there above us all." The idea
is only in our minds.

In our lives we only run into, and have to relate to, the
religions of specific individual people, organizations, or movements. The religions we meet are always concrete; they are
always embodied in those people, movements, and institutions. They're never some *thing* up there, out there, over
there, or outside of the religious people who are embedded in
the personal circumstances of their lives.

We often think and talk in generalizations that are based
upon our experiences of the specific examples we run into in
our lives — but this is not religion in general. And it's not religion in general that believes or does anything at all.

It's the people we meet, read about, and watch on TV whose
religious positions we experience. These people, groups, and
institutions act their religions out on themselves and others
based upon their own understandings and experiences of

what religion is, which are in turn based in their particular experiences with their parents' or other people's religions. The same is true for the usual religions we think of as well. These have often been called the "major world religions."

Yet, there's no such thing in human experience as a disembodied Christianity, Judaism, Islam, Buddhism, or any of the other religions we might list in general either — even paganism, atheism, or agnosticism. We always have to relate to particular movements, scriptures, institutions, and people in historical and present time when we decide how to deal with, or not deal with, religions.

Religion is, frankly, responsible for nothing. In our everyday lives we always find only religions in particular at work. We can only see, deal with, and respond to the religious activities of particular people, particular institutions, and particular movements.

WE ALWAYS RELATE TO SOMEBODY'S VERSION OF RELIGION

The religion we deal with, whether good or bad is always someone's or some group's understanding of religion. It's always someone's particular interpretation of the world about them, someone's definition of what is traditional, and someone's beliefs about how to treat themselves and others.

The fact that we are dealing with something so tied to particular people and groups of people is crucial. In every single case these understandings people have are caught up in, intermingled with, and affected by the particular circumstances of the religious person's life, their upbringing, their psyches, their relationships, their influences, and their prejudices.

It's Uncle Phil's religion, or Aunt Mary's. It's dad's and mom's. It's St. Joseph's by the Gas Station, or First Baptist Church's of Lemond, Kansas. It's Pope Benedict II's, or Jerry Falwell's or Jimmy Carter's. It's the Southern Baptist Convention's or the Second Vatican Council's.

So, understanding and responding to the religious pronouncements, initiatives, bullying, cajoling, blaming, judging, and pressures of the people who believe their religions are true and required for everyone everywhere isn't about responding to religion or any of the religions in general. It's about responding to the specific people and groups who are proclaiming such pronouncements, pushing their own agenda, defaming and condemning those who disagree, and expecting governments to enforce their sectarian moralities.

We're really dealing with convinced, even prejudiced, people. These are people who may feel they're victimized by secular people. They might be afraid to embrace new ideas. They might be believers who cling to their views of gods, tradition, and scriptures in order not to confront their own internal, personal psychological demons. They might get a lot of attention, camaraderie, and community from their like-believing friends for their beliefs and actions, or they might just not want to embrace change because it scared them. The list of factors that affect these believers could go on and on.

The issues we must deal with when we talk about religion are individual and community issues. These issues are often hidden behind some generalization that even they make about true "Christianity," or "religion," or "faith." Yet these issues are very personal and particular.

These are issues that relate to how religion works in and for particular people. They are about how individual religions function to motivate people to do the good and the bad they do.

It's not about the traditions and teachings people were born into, but why different people relate and respond differently to those same traditions and teachings. If it were about religion in general, there'd be little variation in the human responses to the religions of the culture of their youth. However, that's not the case even with siblings from the same religious families.

We've seen it ourselves. Any two people can be born into and raised in the same religious teachings. Some accept the religious teachings. Some reject them. Some interpret them in a variety of ways. Most choose among the teachings and practices which to embrace, which to ignore, or even which to completely discard. Religions function differently in the lives of different people and the groups toward which these people gravitate.

Focusing on these other issues and identifying the ways religion functions in people's lives provides a way to think about why and how people brought up in the same traditions, denominations, and cultures respond differently to the cultural systems they've inherited.

Why do some who were immersed in the Southern, fundamentalist, Protestant Christianity in which they were raised seem to take comfort in the teaching of an eternal, abusive damnation in the after-life for those who disagree, while others raised in the same tradition are inclusive and believe such a concept of hell is abusive and that a loving God would treat no human being that way?

Why do some Southern fundamentalist minister's children become Wiccans while others join White supremacist groups?

Why do some people raised in that religious tradition rail continuously against accepting people of different sexual orientations, while others embrace gay people and believe it's biblical teaching that motivated them to affirm love wherever it's attempted?

Why did many argue that the Bible supported slavery, and later segregation, while others challenged the Biblical verses that kept slaves in their place and found a new understanding of those same verses?

Why do some Baptists today want government support for their religious crusades while others take a more traditional Baptist stand for a "wall of separation" between all religion and the government, and even join groups such as Americans United for the Separation of Church and State to protect that wall?

When we examine addictive religion, then, we're saying nothing about religion in general. We are talking about how religion functions for a large group of people in the United States (and elsewhere), and how the non-addictive, religious or not, can respond to the addiction so as not to enable religious addiction or enmesh themselves in the addictions of others.

CHANGING OUR THINKING ABOUT RELIGIOUSLY ADDICTED PEOPLE

(1) To understand what I am identifying as religion functioning for people as an addiction, those of us outside the addiction first need to see these people in a way that's different from how they see themselves.

We must stop looking at them through the lens they use. They see through the colored glasses of their addiction, and that has them speaking for everything other than their own personal opinions about religion.

We must frankly accept the fact that the very lens addicts use to interpret the world is a distorted one. Addiction specialist, medical doctor, and rabbi Abraham Twerski observes that "addictive thinking" may even look reasonable on the surface. Many people may be taken in by it. But it's actually what Alcoholics Anonymous calls stinkin' thinkin'.

"I cannot stress enough the importance of realizing that addicts are taken in by their own distorted thinking and that they are its victims," Twerski writes in *Addictive Thinking: Understanding Self-Deception*. "If we fail to understand this, we may feel frustrated or angry in dealing with the addict."

The non-addicted usually scratch their heads wondering how the addict can think that way, ignore certain consequences of the addiction, or dismiss what someone outside the addiction considers common sense. Addictive thinking, we must recognize, is not about understanding reality, but is thinking that's meant to keep the addiction going.

So, we must be the ones who see that what they say doesn't speak for anything (religion, Christianity, you name it.) other than themselves. Even though they may claim and even think otherwise, they certainly don't speak for God, scriptures, or tradition. They may speak for a group of people who agree with them, for a way they learned to use in order to make sense of their world, for the official pronouncements of a denomination, or for a movement, but nothing greater.

(2) This means that we are not dealing with religion, God, the Bible, tradition, or anything greater.

We don't have to believe or feel guilty that we are responding to anything greater, because that's not what we are confronting when we deal with religious people. Our discussions with them, disagreements, or any other ways we choose to deal or not deal with them, relate solely to their issues. **We are only dealing with them.**

They may rant and insist otherwise, they may threaten eternal punishment for our disagreement or for the variety of lifestyles we may live that don't conform to their ideas. But it's *their* rant, *their* ideas, *their* belief that they are sinners, *their* need to believe in hell, and *their* particularity that's at issue.

No matter what they say, no matter how what they claim may distract us from this fact, we are not confronting tradition, history, the Bible, the American way, the Judeo-Christian tradition, or any other larger idea. We are looking at their own understanding of life and how they use religion in their particular lifestyle.

(3) This means that we can still consider them whole, worthwhile, and complete people somewhere down deep no matter how religion functions for them.

How we see religion functioning in someone's life for good or ill is a different question than who we personally believe they are as fellow human beings. In fact, our own beliefs about human nature may be kinder on them than their belief in their own inherent sinfulness is.

A young man came up my driveway while I was washing my car one summer day. His purpose, it quickly appeared, was to evangelize me by trying to convince me of his belief that all human beings are inherently evil and, therefore, need saving. That's "what the Bible says," he proclaimed.

I didn't doubt that this was certainly his belief about what the Bible claimed, but I wasn't interested in dealing with the Bible at that point. I had an M.A. in Biblical Studies from a conservative seminary. I knew the arguments for and against his interpretation.

The real key to what he was saying, it seemed, would be better found in how this understanding he fervently embraced spoke of his own beliefs about his own personal vileness. So, since his phrase "all human beings" obviously included himself, I didn't doubt his belief and decided to get down to the personal specifics.

"Then, it looks as if I like you better than you like yourself," was intentionally my only response. "Too bad for you, huh?"

We don't have to assume that people for whom religion is an addiction are inherently evil or anything of the sort. We can see them as people speaking and crusading, or ranting and judging others, mostly out of their own personal experience. Their words and actions often demonstrate to us a lot about what has happened to them.

People, we know, instead of doing the difficult work of facing their own pasts, getting in touch with how they've been hurt, and growing beyond their pain, often get stuck in the numerous mechanisms their families and society made available to them to skirt their issues. These are often addictive uses of substances and processes. Assisting people not to face their own personal issues by focusing their attention upon another issue entirely — God, the Bible, tradition, the Church, precisely correct theology — is a key function of addictive religion.

(4) When religious people speak negatively about other groups, such as non-believers, people of other religions, LGBT people, feminists, or others whom they demonize, they're displaying for all to see what they refuse to confront in their own lives.

It could be past actions, guilt, insecurities, shame, unworthiness, failed relationships, unfulfilled sexual lives, or an inability to embrace their sexual orientation. **We cannot know** as long as they deny, suppress, or refuse to examine these issues. And it's seldom worth our time obsessing about what their personal and emotional issues really are.

How often, for example have we heard of a religious leader known for his obsessively judgmental crusade against other people's sexuality, getting arrested for the public solicitation of sex? How often a crusader against some activity, exposed as addicted to another?

They'll often repeat the language of their punitive parents in their sermonizing and scolding. So, listen carefully to their words and tone.

It's not surprising that televangelists and their political buddies often sound like punishing fathers. Other people who haven't dealt emotionally with their own father issues (much less faced the possibility that they even have them) will be hooked by such talk.

(5) Knowing that this isn't about religion, we also know it's not about the people whom they may attack, scapegoat, and condemn.

The use of religion in this fashion is really about those who are addicted and how religion is functioning in their lives. Projecting their problems on others or on religion, Christianity, or God in abstraction is merely a common way to cope with their issues.

Religion itself becomes a scapegoat in this process. It takes the blame for the addicted person's issues

It's like the alcoholic's excuse for any negative behavior: "It's the alcohol talking." It's excusing actions because "he was drunk at the time." It's the fact that others don't support him.

For those who refuse to face their own issues, it's the religion's fault. But it's never them as individuals or the personal issues they would have to examine and face if they took responsibility.

(6) This, then, is the addictive *use* of religion, an addiction that we are about to examine further.

It's a process addiction where religion is used, I am arguing, like drugs and alcohol, or other even good activities and substances. Religion is depended upon to prevent the addicts from facing real personal issues. It's mood-altering. That's why those outside the addiction can't get caught enabling addictive religion, especially by arguing about an abstract, disembodied thing called religion, Christianity, or any other religion, in general.

We must choose to stop arguing about religion or blaming religion before we even begin. When we blame religion, Christianity, or particular brands of religion and spend our time arguing against religion in general, we actually keep the addiction going. When we argue this way, we are on the addictive turf of the addicts themselves, just where they would like the argument to be.

We're thereby enabling the addicts to whine that they're the real victims in all this. They are being discriminated against because they are religious, or because of their beliefs. It's become a common response of the religiously addicted: "We're the victims." And whining is a substitute for recovery from an addiction.

Recovery groups confront addicts who don't take personal responsibility in their particular circumstances for their particular addictive behavior with: "Get off the pity pot." It's now up to the rest of us to stop providing the pot for them.

CHAPTER TWO

WILL WE CALL IT ADDICTION?

A now classic Peanuts comic strip pictures blanket-hugging Linus explaining to good ole Charlie Brown: "I love mankind — it's people I can't stand." Linus' distinction between the generalization and particular cases is insightful for relating to the religious people we come across.

To talk about how religion functions as an addiction in people's lives and to identify people as religious addicts is to say nothing either positive or negative about all religions, any specific religions, or religion in general. It's to identify, and then examine, the way specific people, both individually and in groups, use religion to control their lives. It's to recognize how religion — as these people understand and relate to it — helps them cope with the world we all live in in the often mystifying way these individuals define and interpret that world.

Identifying people as religious addicts is no different than finally coming to terms with the realization that alcoholism is a friend's problem. That should change the way we relate to the friend's thinking, words, and actions. But it doesn't condemn the friend or even alcohol itself.

We know this. When people speak disparagingly of a "wino," they're usually not condemning wine. We even know that many researchers have concluded that drinking a glass of red wine every day may be a healthy practice that prevents heart disease.

Over-the-counter and prescription painkillers can be lifesaving substances that are necessary for day-to-day functioning for many people and a relief from occasional physical pain for others when they're used as directed. An aspirin a day is even prescribed by physicians, again for cardio-vascular health.

Addiction to these same drugs, a more common occurrence in our county than we'd like to admit, however, is a sign of disease and personal dysfunction. It tells us these drugs are being used to cover more than any immediate physical pain. Like all addictions, their addictive use is often progressive and even fatal.

Certainly no one in Overeaters Anonymous would conclude from the personal eating problem they've come to terms with, that food in itself is bad for us. What those who join such programs are admitting to themselves is that food functions for them as an addiction, and that eating ("using" it) is compulsive, out of control, and a means of avoiding their deepest insecure feelings. Eating is a process that prevents them from recognizing the past and present hurt and pain they would need to face in order to live healthier, addiction-free, lives.

Some nutritionists do argue that certain ingredients in our food, such as caffeine, sugar, other simple carbohydrates, and food additives are chemically addictive. Yet eating as a ritual-like process and food used as a mood-altering substance can fill someone so full that they can't feel anything but a "comforting" feeling of being full or the miserable "satisfaction" of being stuffed to the gills. On a more benign level, we even refer to menu items that remind us of past good feelings as "comfort food."

Food addiction provides well-known examples of how an addictive obsession to a benign substance can actually manifest itself in obsessively not using the substance — either not eating, or gorging oneself with a huge quantity and then desperately rejecting it. Around 11 million Americans have the anorexia and bulimia that illustrate the obsession of an addiction acting out in ways that actually reject the substance itself.

Yet, indulging and/or obsessively rejecting it means that

it's still the substance food that is controlling their lives. Food, or other substances and processes used as the anorexic or bulimic uses food, still becomes central to an addict's way of functioning in the world.

MORE THAN JUST ALCOHOL AND DRUGS

Addiction specialists recognize both substance and process addictions. The first category is more widely accepted as addictions and more widely recognized as personal problems. These are the substance or ingestive addictions such as alcohol, drugs, nicotine, caffeine, and food. Alcoholics Anonymous, Narcotics Anonymous, Overeaters Anonymous, and Rational Recovery are established programs meant to help people in recovery from such substance addictions.

The most difficult barrier to recognizing and dealing with our own or someone else's addiction is the practiced denial and deception that keeps us from facing the addiction. That's why the step that begins recovery programs like AA even before one begins the famous 12 Steps is to introduce oneself unequivocally as addicted. Recovery begins with a courageous recognition to others in a meeting and to oneself through hearing oneself say out loud: "Hi. I'm Bob. And I'm an alcoholic."

Breaking through the self-denial is difficult enough to do with substance addictions even though recovery programs such as AA, NA, and RR are well-known and mainstreamed. Such substance abuse programs are recognized, affirmed, and promoted by our cultural system even while the system promotes the legal sales of more alcohol, drugs, and food to help people cope with the human problems inherent to the system itself. The cultural debate is over which model to use to understand these addictions — disease, brain chemical disorder, genetic problems, cognitive failures, or behavioral based problems — but addictions they are.

There's no broad-based commercial worry that available recovery programs might threaten the profitable sales of alcohol, potentially addictive drugs, and other substances that are sold by our profit-oriented industries and used by addicts. By their very charters AA, NA, OA, and RR assure the suppliers and the rest of us that they won't take on the larger systemic causes that call for addictions. They won't threaten the nature of our institutions, or the legal pushers themselves.

Nicotine addiction might be a potential exception, since local governments are restricting the locations where it can be used, and the variety of its delivery systems. Non-smoking ordinances are spreading to control one of the most addictive legal substances with its highly efficient delivery system, while the tobacco industry is counting on ever-new markets at home and overseas.

Since alcohol and drug manufacturers and distributors don't see AA, NA, OA, or RR as posing a threat to their huge profits in the marketplace or to other institutions of American culture, these substance addictions can be openly recognized as addictions that only need treatment in what we are to believe is a small minority of their users. Some of the very industries that profit from alcohol, tobacco, and drug sales even support such treatment programs.

Additionally, when the addictions are interpreted as diseases of an individual's body chemistry, the pharmaceutical industry itself can tap a potential source of more profits with the development and promotion of drugs for "treating" these diseases. An industry of profit-oriented treatment centers is ready and waiting for addicts and their funds to pour in.

TAKING PROCESS ADDICTIONS SERIOUSLY

As a recognized category, process addictions are less mainstream. There is widespread denial that such addictions even exist or, more commonly, that any particular individual is seriously addicted to any of the processes.

The numerous cultural institutions that have become dependent themselves on process addictions fuel both types of denial. Even where the idea of the existence of process addictions is embraced within a society, these addictions are often minimized, winked at, or ridiculed.

Substance addictions are usually defined by professionals as addictions or "substance abuse" (to use the language of *The Diagnostic and Statistical Manual of Mental Disorders, Fourth Edition* of the American Psychiatric Association) when they interfere with "major role obligations," are used persistently in physically or legally hazardous situations, or cause or exacerbate "persistent or recurrent social or interpersonal problems" centering upon the use of the addictive substance itself.

This definition of "substance abuse" indicates to the psychiatric community when the use of a substance rises to the level of a mental disorder. The question this definition turns upon is how something impairs one's activities in a world where process addictions may actually not interfere, but promote, the "roles" people are expected to live to maintain the functioning of the socio-economic system as it is. For many, then, the use of a substance is not labeled "abuse" if it doesn't interfere with the efficient work of American commerce, even though it may hide other significant personal problems within the abuser.

At the end of a workshop I was leading for a group of state social workers, we talked about working with men in our culture to promote their healing, not just giving up on men by assuming that men are "that way." It's often still assumed that men are almost hopelessly testosterone driven, angry, violent, sexual predators, and that all one can do is cope with that through management, medication, or incarceration if their problems rise to the level of offending the larger community.

These seasoned social work veterans, however much they supported the personal growth of their clients and saw that men are actually full human beings, reminded me that their job was not to promote client healing but to see that their clients "fit in." Their assigned task was to ensure that the homeless didn't wander the streets offending the rest of us, that the chronically mentally ill didn't bother others, that the disabled didn't look too pitiful to the able-bodied, and that the addicted were in programs that kept them out of crime and their addictions out of sight.

Social workers have often been one of the least respected professionals within medical teams — just compare their salaries to all the others. Yet they are the ones who must struggle most closely with everyday human problems in the dirt, grime, disease, and poverty of human lives. The realism of these professionals about employer and societal expectations wasn't mere cynicism but the result of their experiences in a system that was geared to keeping itself going — a system that they recognized was profit-oriented, not human-oriented, and coping-oriented, not healing-oriented.

Process addictions illicit more indifference than substance addictions. Our current socio-economic system has developed a ravenous appetite for growth and expansion that has become dependent upon these process addictions. They're crucial to maintaining a dysfunctional pace. Addictions useful to the promotion of economic development, growth, and expansion must not be considered seriously as addictions that have the same patterns, problems, and human toll as substance addictions.

To identify and embrace the ideas that these activities are addictions and that they are as serious as substance addictions, poses a threat to the cultures and processes of some of the very institutions that succeed because these addictions exist. It's easier to deny the existence of process addictions, ignore them, write them off, laugh at them, or define them so abstractly that the majority of us don't need to question whether we too might be caught up in these addictions of process.

Gambling has become a major activity of the "entertainment" industry. We can't say that the majority of those who gamble do so as an addiction. Yet, we've also come to embrace the idea that there is a gambling addiction, even if we don't want to admit its magnitude.

State governments even mandate that the gambling industry itself support programs for such addicts. They even give the addicts toll-free numbers to call when they end their denial of the addiction — though most who are addicted will continue to gamble. And these governments themselves, with support of some of the most conservative, moralistically anti-taxation lawmakers, have become dependent upon the gambling industry for monetary support.

The now mainstreamed industry has even changed what it calls itself to the "gaming" industry. That new name escapes many of the negative, even seedy, connotations gambling accrued in the US, while it separates the activity of "gaming" from the addiction ("gambling") and from recovery groups such as Gamblers Anonymous. The process is thereby mainstreamed with growth in government revenues dependent upon those who are addicted to the process but don't recognize their addiction.

We talk about workaholism and workaholics who over-work, spend little time with their spouses and children, and center their lives around their work — who live to work not merely work to live. We even remind ourselves, with a wink and a chuckle, that no one ever says on their deathbed: "I sure wish that I'd have spent more time at the office."

Yet we do little about workaholism's specific addicts or the conditions that promote it because our economic system requires an addiction to work with a "yes" attitude in order for it to expand at the rapid pace to which our investment industry has become addicted. It's better to deny the extent of this addiction.

How many times do US economists measure a nation's success not in terms of the health of its workers, the amount of time they spend with their families, the quality of their leisure, or their sense of fulfillment in their work? It's measured instead by US economic productivity (the GNP and GDP, the DOW Jones, and the S&P) and the rapidity of overall economic growth. So great is our dependence upon (our addiction to?) fast-paced growth that we even use words like "recession" and "stagnation" not to mean that the overall economy isn't growing at all but that it's not growing fast enough.

In the US, European economies are often compared less favorably to the US as if these countries are failing to be successful as nations because their emphasis is upon health, satisfaction, family and vacation time, and a sense of not being alienated from one's work, even at the expense of slower overall economic growth. Americans work more hours, have less time with their families, have far less vacation time, and are then often valued because they are "more productive" than those in the European Union.

A 2003 Boston College study found that 26% of US workers take no vacation time at all. A May Conference Board poll determined that 40% of Americans had no plans to take a vacation during 2006.

Work in itself can be one important way to express our humanity and promote the humane growth and success of others. It can be fulfilling when it helps people live out of their core spiritual and moral values. Yet working often becomes compulsive, an activity in which to hide so as not to deal with self-identity, relationship, meaningfulness, or family problems.

Many who are addicted to their work find more comfort, support, and meaning at the job and from their fellow workers than they do at home or even in their religious institutions. "We're like a family here," is a not uncommon claim many corporate executives take pride in touting. And when relationships at work begin to become more fulfilling than those at home, it's easier to emotionally and physically "cheat" on those at home.

Living in retirement is difficult for workaholics because their work was the center of their world. The alternative of centering one's life elsewhere is too radical a change that's accompanied by withdrawal symptoms.

And of course the more one works, the more one earns. The system's rewards are in cold cash. Who would have ever thought that American workers would consider overtime a benefit – the "privilege" of working even more hours to make ends meet?

Societal and individual denial that someone is addicted to these and other processes is a normal cultural condition. This denial of the existence and the destructiveness of process addictions became an important target of the argument of addiction specialist Ann Wilson Schaef in her 1987 best-seller, *When Society Becomes an Addict* and in her co-authored 1988 follow-up work with the descriptive title: *The Addictive Organization: Why We Overwork, Cover Up, Pick Up the Pieces, Please the Boss and Perpetuate Sick Organizations.*

The current US socioeconomic-cultural system itself, Schaef argued, is in fact an "addictive system" that needs addictions to function. It teaches us to live in addictive processes as if they are normal. That doesn't condemn society, just as alcoholism doesn't condemn alcohol, but it describes the overall approach to the world that American society has developed and the nature of our society's current demands upon us.

Since that's the case, Schaef observed, both substance and process addictions are essential to the culture: "Addictions take the edge off, block awareness that could threaten our seeming equilibrium and allow us to grow, and keep us too busy to challenge the system."

WHEN A PROCESS BECOMES AN ADDICTION

Growing scientific evidence shows that the brain can react in the same way to processes as it does to commonly recognized addictive substances. Studies of a number of activities have already indicated that reactions in the human brain involving messenger chemicals such as dopamine occur just as they do with alcohol and drugs. Activities can produce the same pleasurable high that addicts seek through their abuse of a substance.

Major research university studies have documented these reactions for gambling, pursuit of financial gain, and even political activities that reinforced ones prejudices. Not all those engaged in these activities show the same "pleasure" effect. Like substance addiction, the difference is likely to be how an activity becomes the means to relieve personal pain, suffering, threats to self-esteem, and distress.

A process becomes an addiction when the process becomes the center of life, the most important reason for living, when a person becomes dependent upon the process for mood-altering relief from the rest of life. For someone addicted to a process, the process with all its using activities substitutes for taking actions that would change the circumstances of one's personal life and society that demand addictions to relieve the distress.

Instead of changing their boring, demeaning, or psychologically or physically deadly working conditions or the corporate-dominated society that sets them, the person becomes dependent for escape in what may be otherwise healthy activities. Instead of dealing with the issues of a difficult marriage or other relationships, loneliness or meaninglessness, the person becomes dependant for relief by participating in, or becoming a fan of, repetitive activities that provide "entertainment" and escape.

The person becomes, as Schaef puts it, "hooked on a process — a specific series of actions or interactions." Whether the process is any one of those she enumerates — accumulating money, gambling, sex, work, religion, or worry — there is nothing about these activities in themselves that means they must become addictive.

Yet, they become addictive when our life revolves around them, not around our deepest selves, our closest relationships, and our humanity. They take control of us while all the while we believe that we're in control. We go to them for nurturing and relief. We spend our time thinking of how to practice more of them and looking forward to them even in the middle of other activities that should receive our undivided attention.

Process addicts believe all the while that they're in control, that they haven't let the process hurt their lives or injure their closest relationships, just as non-recovering alcoholics believe they are in control of their lives and can quit at any time. It's not surprising that an early step in recovery programs is to ask oneself what power the addiction has over me. **Process addictions also provide a "high" for the addict.** They're mood-altering. The high process addictions produce could actually be chemically discernible in the brain, but it's a high that the addicted one relies upon to "prove" that they are more, that is better, than what the rest of everyday life otherwise tells them they are.

It's the high of a process upon which one becomes dependent and, thus, on the process that produces that high. Hence, *The Diagnostic and Statistical Manual of Mental Disorders* of the American Psychiatric Association in its definition of addictions observes: "Essentially, addiction designates a process whereby a behavior, that can function both to produce pleasure and to provide escape from internal discomfort, is employed in a pattern characterized by (1) recurrent failure to control the behavior (powerlessness) and (2) continuation of the behavior despite significant negative consequences (unmanageability)."

The high of the addiction is fleeting, causing those dependent upon it to seek further and greater "fixes," further experiences of that high. The mood-altering feelings don't last. The addiction lets the addict down and requires further and more intense fixes to get the addict up again. So, repetition of the momentary experiences of relief that the high brings from an otherwise disappointing life becomes the often hidden goal. In this way, addictions are progressive.

There is never enough money to feel great. When the addicted have earned the money they sought, the high wears off. They feel less safe again, more threatened. So, on to accumulating even more money, for that feels more and more necessary to restore the high that relieves all the other undesirable feelings and fears.

The sex is never enough to do it for an addict; the high is too fleeting, the mental chemistry of the climax doesn't last. More sex becomes necessary, multiple partners, or a partner other than the current one who will finally be able to give the sexaholic that more intense high.

Though workaholics might get great feelings from work accomplished, no amount of work is finally ever enough. The feelings don't last. Fear sets in that they haven't done enough work. There's always more that must be done to feel better about oneself.

WAIT, NOW. I'M NOT ADDICTED!

There are two requirements for keeping any addiction going. The first is the denial in the mind of the addict that the addict is really an addict.

For process addictions, the denial we must first break through is a broader cultural denial. For example, only within the last fifteen years have addiction specialists been able to convince the larger culture that there is such a condition as sexual addiction. A claim that earlier produced responses of suspicion and a spate of jokes, had become professionally recognized, for example, in the late 1990s with the inclusion of chapters on sexual addiction in three basic medical texts in 1997.

If we could get past such cultural denial, we'd see process addictions differently. Then the addicted one must get through the personal denial that they themselves are addicted.

The addictions cause us to think and do things that might otherwise be inconsistent with our deepest intuitions and humane feelings. They separate us from activities and attitudes that promote honest relationships and express the personal values that arise from within.

They lead to self-deception. While submersed in the addiction, we tell ourselves all is okay and we're in control.

Like substance addictions, process addictions substitute the "message" of the addiction for the other messages inside us. In themselves, they keep us from being aware of and really feeling what is going on inside.

These addictions come with messages that tell us how we *should* feel instead of affirming how we *do* feel.

We *should* feel good about our work, no matter how exhausting.

We *should* rejoice in our religion, no matter how awful we feel about ourselves, how difficult it is to understand "God's ways," and how scared we feel about our future in the afterlife.

We *should* want more sex ("Hey, it's natural to feel that way!") no matter how disappointing it is to us.

Our own emotional reactions must be ignored, buried, and rejected. It's best if we become so out of touch with how we really feel that we don't even know what the feelings would be without the intrusion of the addiction. The process itself provides a mental justification for how we should feel instead and condemns alternative intuitions, insights, and emotions.

Twerski argues that an addict's denial is actually an unconscious self-deception: "Virtually all of an addict's defense mechanisms are unconscious, and their function is to protect the addict from some intolerable, unacceptable, and catastrophic awareness."

This self-deception leads to deceiving others, particularly those in the closest relationships with the addict. We don't want others to see who we're afraid we really are.

We're tempted to jest, exaggerate, tell partial truths, and lie even to those who could be the most supportive. We begin to lie to cover up the addictiveness of the process in our lives. The lie comes to feel like a justifiable strategy as if others don't deserve the truth, or are too deficient or unable to handle it.

When religion, for example, is an addiction, it becomes easier to deceive in the name of the addiction. Religious addicts believe that almost any means will justify the end, which is defending and spreading the Truth. The dishonesty isn't, addicts believe, really dishonest. The end — promoting our religion, getting others to agree with us — justifies the means.

"There is an insidious quality about religious addiction and the abuse it spawns," John Bradshaw writes in his forward to Leo Booth's *When God Is a Drug*. "The denial of religious addicts is the most delusional denial of all addictions. Delusion means 'sincere denial.'"

As addicted ones lose contact with themselves, they lose contact with others. Others become like objects useable for the addiction. Addicts define others in terms of the addiction not as they would define themselves. They become out of touch with how what they are doing is affecting, even hurting, those around them.

Recovery groups recognize what they call "the con," the addict's ability to manipulate others all the while protesting that the addict is sincere. Those around the addict, of course, want to give the addicted one the benefit of the doubt and are hoping for the best. So, they believe the addict is sincere. That makes it easier for the addict to con them.

In the end, though, the addict blames others for the addict's problems. Scapegoats are everywhere. No personal responsibility is accepted for either the existence or results of the addiction. The problems of the addict's life are all the fault of a spouse, partners, friends, co-workers, the boss, the children, one's parents — anyone and anything but the addict and their addiction.

Addicts can even become angry and righteously indignant about the problems they blame for the addiction. It's really other people's problems, the demands of the boss, the spouse, the children, the world, life, fate, luck, bad religion, even God.

Alcoholics, for example, take a drink to make them feel better. Without the drink, the negative emotions might be overwhelming. And there seems to be no other alternative than the drink. One would have to face and do something to end the boredom and demeaning of the work one does most waking hours, or a marriage that is routine and unfulfilling, or friendships one feels are with people who don't really know the real person inside.

The drink provides the altered mood, the high that becomes a means of survival in a world that is otherwise experienced as boring, disappointing, unfulfilling, painful, and even, maybe, out to get her or him, a world from which there is no exit. It helps one relax, let the burdens of life go away for a little while, and even numb one to the pain of it all.

There's an isolation to all this as if no one else would understand. The others all seem to be doing well. Not talking about it seems to be the best strategy while it keeps one feeling alone in the midst of the crowd.

Talking to anyone about these things would be seen to be weakness, whining, feeling sorry for oneself, and acting like a failure who can't cut it. To be seen by others this way comes with punishments that reinforce the silence about how it might all feel — loss of friendships, one's job, one's significant other, one's reputation, and one's future.

Then there's the ideology of the addiction that's repeated again and again until it has taken on the aura of truth. It says that heavy drinking is acceptable and even sociable. There's something weird, even funny about someone who doesn't drink. Alcohol is expected at social gatherings. "Come on," the ideology goes, "loosen up, have a drink. You'll feel better. We all do it. One drink won't hurt you. You're a social drinker, not some skid row drunk."

All of this prevents the addict from accepting the addiction. Denial is easier. Recovery is difficult work.

I'M NOT ENABLING. I'M BEING COMPASSIONATE.

The second requirement for maintaining an addiction is the enabling of the addiction by those around the addict. Those around the addict, particularly those most enmeshed in the addict's life, usually fall into a pattern that addiction specialists often call "co-addiction."

They are the enablers. Their actions enable the addict to not experience the negative consequences of the addiction. They make endless excuses, cover up, blame themselves, try harder, walk on eggshells, and refuse to call the addiction an addiction. Enabling thereby helps the addict remain in denial.

It has become an established assumption among addiction researchers and therapists, with thousands of articles documenting the fact, that addiction is a family illness. Families of addicts, however, resist greatly the idea that they too need to face the reality that part of the problem is their own codependency or co-addiction.

They have convinced themselves that they are being nice and understanding. Yet they continue to obsess about the addict's behavior, blame themselves for what's happening, and attempt to control or fix the addict. All of this, addiction specialists say, simply makes the problem worse.

The addict's spouse enables the addiction when she or he makes excuses for the addict, calls an employer to cover for the addict's absences, "explains" the addict's reasons for "not feeling well" to their children, refuses to believe the drunk is a drunk, blames themself for the addict's problems, wants to be nice rather than honest, is afraid to offend the addict while the addiction occupies the center of the family's life, and adjusts the home life to "please" the addict. Friends, as well, prefer to make excuses rather than threaten their friendships.

An addiction cannot exist without the enablers who are often, in often strange ways, dependent upon the addict for their livelihood, feelings of worth, and meaning. The enablers don't want to upset the addict.

They know that calling the person an alcoholic or drug addict is guaranteed to trigger the addict's anger. They're right, of course.

Addicts don't want to hear that they are addicts, will most

likely get angry, and even possibly attack verbally or physically anyone who says they are. They'll do anything to deny
their addiction and to project the blame and their issues onto
others.

It would be a perfectly appropriate, healthy action for the
little child in an alcoholic family to push open the door of his
or her parents' bedroom and demand: "Dad, you go to AA.
Mom, get in Al Anon. If not, I'm out of this family."

There is certainly, however, a practical reason for the child
not to do so. Children, after all, are dependent upon their parents for survival.

But adult enablers are seldom really dependent for their
survival on the addict. Enabling an addict is usually a result
of the enabler's own unfaced problems. It stifles the life of the
enabler. Instead of living their own life on their own terms for
themselves, it keeps the enabler living a life defined by the
addiction.

Ending the patterns of enabling is also difficult. Doing so
goes against all the messages we've absorbed from society
that say we should do everything to be nice. We don't want
to offend the addict even though the addict offends us and
everyone around them.

As members of Al-Anon know, there are "three C's"
enablers must remember: You did not Cause it, you cannot
Control it, and you cannot Cure it. But we can and must confront it. It's called intervention.

**Enablers, then, must change their strategies, not to
change the addict but for their own health and sanity.**
Ultimately, the addict might also benefit.

CHAPTER THREE
THE "HIGH" OF RIGHTEOUSNESS

I remember hearing John Bradshaw explain that the "high" someone gets from feeling righteous is similar to the high of cocaine. It was one of those "ah-hah" moments. As he described the two further, what began as surprising but also in line with my own thinking about religious addiction, made even more sense.

Bradshaw's comparison of the highs of two addictions was both personally and socially courageous. He spoke from personal experience, he said, for he was not only a counselor but also a former monk and a recovering addict who knew how both denial and enabling keep addictions going.

It also took courage to examine honestly and openly the emotion of righteousness that often the most visible and powerful religious people cherish. His was an observation about the function religion has in many people's lives that would provoke controversy. To openly name such a similarity of addictiveness, after all, challenges much of the religious establishment.

Many religious people criticize, condemn, or think of drug addiction as a problem for people far beneath them. So, comparing the emotions of being religiously righteous to a drug-induced high feels threatening to them and their thinking.

And many people wouldn't consider it polite to say such things out loud. So, it's guaranteed to offend many.

BEYOND THE NEED TO BE "NICE"

In their work, Bradshaw and other addiction specialists are emphatic about the importance of plain speaking about addiction in our world even when reactions are likely to be negative. They recognize that an alcoholic in denial will often become angry if called a drunk. Moving into the alcoholic's anger, in fact, allows alcoholics to keep from examining the more painful possibility of the truth that they're addicts.

In a set of taped lectures, for example, Bradshaw spoke about "The Price of Nice," its personal cost to a person who's been taught not to speak their truth because: "It isn't nice. It will offend people." Instead, "nice people" have learned to feel they must be polite and nonoffending at all costs even if being "nice" enables an addiction and destroys their families, themselves, and others around the addict.

Though it might actually be a courageous expression of "tough love," many people just wouldn't consider it "nice" to describe the feeling of righteousness as a "high" that is evidence of something called religious addiction. Not only might it offend the addicts, but other nice "liberals," who themselves constantly endure being offended by the addicts' words and actions, will blush and object, distancing themselves from anyone who speaks such words.

"Be nice," can be an unhealthy internalized command to obey when one's own and society's health is at stake. As I heard filmmaker Michael Moore once say, "I'm not a liberal. I don't have to be nice." Notice how often liberals distance themselves from Moore for that very reason.

They want to be nice. They want to protect everybody's feelings, even those of people who speak openly of these same liberals as terrorists.

Liberal people get scared because they know how bad they'd feel if someone called them addicts. They have, however, been called much worse by right-wing politicians, talk show hosts, and fundamentalist preachers. Yet they don't want to feel bad personally or be accused of making other people feel bad.

M. Scott Peck in *A World Waiting to be Born: Civility Rediscovered*, argues that we will not return to civility in our culture if we think in terms of practicing politeness and good manners at all costs. Manners and polite conversation usually, he says, don't promote truth but "are designed to avoid hurting people's feelings."

In contrast to worrying about hurting someone's feelings, Peck argues, true civility requires that we focus upon and value awareness and our conscious intentions in what we do and say. Thus, he finds a profound insight, which he returns to again and again, in the words of Oliver Herford: "A gentleman is one who never hurts anyone's feelings unintentionally."

"I'm sorry you're offending people and not respecting their beliefs. It's not appropriate. There may be some of those people here and we want them to feel welcome," someone wrote on a liberal discussion board in response to a post about calling addictive religion an addiction.

The respondent, worried about "offending people," couldn't embrace the recovery group principle that allowing people to face such negative emotions is the real point. Making excuses for them and acting out of the fear of offending addicts are the marks of people who enable addictions.

THE RELIEF OF A RIGHTEOUS HIGH

When in the 1960s the so-called "Jesus movement" and young, self-styled "Jesus freaks" preached that people should get "high on Jesus," not on drugs, they personally recognized the similarities of religious and drug experiences. "Jesus" was the drug that replaced the high of the hallucinogenic drugs they had experienced. At the same time there were others who, instead of embracing a Jesus high, argued that drug-induced highs themselves, like that from LSD, were actually religious experiences.

It makes sense, then, that people who are addicted to substances or processes often trade the high of those addictions for the high of being righteous. What's been called conversion or being "born again" actually can be a substitution of one addiction for another. Addiction specialists recognize such a shift as often a type of relapse they call "cross addiction."

"If you go back and trace the course of early recovery for those people," Henderson observes, "you often find that the emotional, psychological, and spiritual aspects of the addiction were not completely addressed. They have been 'white knuckling' and continue to have problems coping with painful emotions."

The convert maintains the same addictive thinking as before. There's a similar level of intensity in their dependence upon religion as their dependence upon the previous addiction. And the substitution will remain successful as long as the religion continues to produce a more fulfilling high than the substance or process they had abandoned.

Like the experience of the high in other addictions, the high of being righteous and on the side of goodness and the Divine numbs one against the worries, insecurities, threats, and pain of other life experiences. It's so appealing because it's a fleeting place for the "righteous" one to feel better.

The high affirms momentarily the rightness, goodness, and acceptability of the believer by no less than the Universe itself. And it distances believers from those other unrighteous people whom they would otherwise experience as threatening, as sinners who could challenge the religious and moralistic beliefs that the religious believe save them.

"I know I'm on the side of the Truth here," a young self-identified conservative Christian man said recently. "This is God's word and it's so great to know that you're on God's side. You don't know the joy, the exhilaration, the high. It's really the joy of the Lord."

The religiously addicted become dependent on the high for repeated relief from the negativity of life and feelings about themselves. This dependency keeps them attached to the religious process that produces the high as long as the process brings the fix.

With religious addiction, the failure to continue in the high is usually blamed on lack of faith in the addict. Faith, of course, is a crucial element for most religious people — faith in God,

faith in the teachings of a preacher, prophet, guru or bud-
dha, faith in organizations and leaders, faith in scriptures and
traditions. This religious emphasis upon the need to believe
enforces the idea that the high is still available to the addict
even when the addict fails to achieve it.

Failure to continue in the high is seen as a symptom of the
addict's faltering faith, not a problem inherent in the addictive
process. It's a problem with them that's about who they are,
not the addiction or its pushers. So even more acts of faith are
necessary, more of the religious process.

In circular fashion, the demand for such faith reinforces
dependence on the high, the fix of religious addiction. It makes
the search for the high to prove that one does have this valuable thing called faith even more desperate. It thereby also
makes religious addiction harder to abandon.

MEDICATING THE LOWEST OF LOW SELF-CONCEPTS

The fix provided by the righteous high not only provides a
feeling of relief from the dangers that the religious person sees
in the world around them. In the case of right-wing religion,
it's also a relief from the nagging emotional consequences of
a central conservative Christian doctrine that for the right-
wing defines the cause of all of the evil that's in the world. It's
a doctrine that's crucial for the success of right-wing religion
because once someone personally accepts it, then the way
has been smoothly paved for embracing the solution that conservative Christianity offers.

It's a religious doctrine that undergirds the dominant
understanding of human nature throughout the United States.
Its long history can be traced back to the Puritans, their
European ancestors in the Protestant Reformation and Roman
Catholicism, and the teachings of the Augustinian version of
Christianity that received the seal of approval of the Imperial
Roman Empire and its Church Councils.

The doctrine is simple and everywhere. Most of us have
embraced it even if we don't identify as right-wing Christians.
But it's especially essential for the success of the Christian

right-wing, no matter what their denominational or nonde-
nominational allegiance.

**Crucial to much religious addiction is the conservative
Christian teaching that people are basically so evil and lost
that they deserve eternal, unimaginably abusive punishment from someone they are told is really a loving heavenly
Father.** It teaches that the model of love for us all should be
rightly abusive of all of His children, all of us.

There's evidence of the broader popularity of this extremely negative view of human beings in many of our institutions.
It's found in our off-hand references to flawed human nature,
our everyday interpretations about how humans will and do
act, and our valuing of a government that maintains checks
and balances on suspect humans.

Widely accepted aphorisms such as: "Power corrupts and
absolute power corrupts absolutely," are really about our negative expectations of human nature that are hidden behind
an abstract notion of what power is supposed to do to everyone. And since everyone's been hurt by someone, personal
anecdotal evidence is all that many of us need to provide
examples that enforce this pervasive cultural assumption of
humanity's evil bent. We move effortlessly from the observation that people often *do* "bad" things to the conviction that
people, in fact, *are* bad.

The popularity of the fundamentalist belief about human
evilness in the US tells us much about the society we live in.
Though it's often spoken of unemotionally as some abstract,
impersonal principle or doctrine — "all human nature is sinful" — its effect is very personal and difficult to shake off.

It would feel shameful to admit this of ourselves, particularly in detail, and especially if we're religious leaders. We'd
rather not think about it too deeply or dwell on its emotional
meaning for too long. We'd prefer to move our thoughts on as
quickly as possible to something more positive, like the hope
that we've been "saved" from the consequences of our sordid
selves.

I've made it my regular response to ask people who tell me that they believe all humans are sinners, evil, depraved, or lost: "Tell me how evil you are. Give me some current examples." It often stops the discussion cold. Who wants to present a current list of their depravity and feel the sense of shame that personalizing the belief raises? It's easier to abstract out of such feelings by talking about humanity and human nature in general.

The very idea that most people would believe that they personally were born totally depraved, in original sin, or flawed beyond the capacity to change things by themselves, is more personal, internalized, and emotional than one would suspect from any abstract theological notion religious thinkers prefer to discuss coldly. What's amazing is that such a doctrine would even appeal to anyone.

It must strike a familiar cord that's already at home within. Otherwise people would reject it as a sick, perverse, insulting, and grotesque idea. It must fit snuggly with the way the majority of children are brought up in our culture that so many would willingly embrace the belief that in themselves they're hopelessly doomed and unquestionably deserving of unending and unspeakably horrible Parental punishment.

Most people were probably prepared for this religious teaching by their personal experiences of dominant Western childrearing methods that punish what parents have been taught are inherently bad children. By these methods, parents teach children to focus their minds on children's mistakes, flaws, errors, and sins. We're to expect sinful behavior as normal and crush it.

Once they fully embrace their personal evilness, such religion takes over their lives by also providing the salvation from their evil selves and from the consequences of their evil selves in the world. Who wouldn't flee desperately to some solution if it promises to replace such negative feelings about oneself?

We cannot find our worth within, period. Someone else,

Fundamentalism says, must prove we're good, since we can't. And that Someone else has no experience of actually being as deeply rotten as we are. He may have tried to be "human" in some way, but without our overriding inborn depravity and sin.

Fortunately though, the doctrine continues, this Someone is inclined to like us in spite of our awful worthlessness, our unacceptability. Even a modern liberal theologian such as Paul Tillich can't shake this dominant sense of unworthiness. He characterized this solution as: "Accepting our acceptance, in spite of the fact that we are unacceptable."

That's the core of conservative and right-wing Christian theology. **It's built not on the idea that its god loves us because we are in ourselves valuable — it believes that would be the sin of pride — but that we in ourselves would have no value at all if its god did not love us.** We are so born, so constituted, it teaches, that the only right and just thing for any just and loving god to do would be to leave us to the unbearable suffering we deserve.

There are attempts to point to another Christian belief that human beings were all originally "created in the image of God," the *imago dei,* but in right-wing Christianity that can't be the final word. It must be followed, without missing a beat, with the claim that this image is broken, fallen, depraved, and far beyond human repair.

The negative teaching trumps any attempts to talk about God's image in human beings because the teaching of *imago dei* is not at the center of the right-wing gospel message that's essential to bringing people into the religion. It's not dwelt upon in the widely-used, well-worn popular evangelism summaries such as: "The Four Spiritual Laws," "The Plan of Salvation," "The Roman Road to Salvation," "How to Be Born Again," "Steps to Peace with God," "How to Get to Heaven," and "Praying the Sinner's Prayer."

Instead, it's necessary for potential converts to internalize the negative teaching about themselves so that they will flee in desperation to the right-wing Christian solution. In this theology, any other thoughts about human nature are peripheral and presented as unemotionally abstract.

They can be discussed later only after the negative belief and emotions have been instilled and the solution accepted. Then the idea of *imago dei* will be discussed along with "correct" subordinating interpretations of it in terms of the more important teaching of "The Fall of Man," "total depravity," "the sinful nature," the Old Man," or "original sin."

It must be emphasized that this essential right-wing doctrine is internalized as no mere claim about some other human being's opinion. No, this is a Divine pronouncement, with all the weight of Divinity behind it. It's the Maker and Judge of the universe who knows that you personally have no basis in who you really are for what psychologists call positive self-esteem.

Even if God, Himself, is going to treat me *as if* I am loveable, the believer learns, God is going to have to reach out to me, as one of America's most popular hymns preaches: "Just as I am without one plea."

Even believing you are, or have been, "saved" still doesn't make you valuable in yourself, after all. You still deserve punishment, and if you don't show the appropriate results ("fruit") of "salvation" as defined by each particular religion, that might indicate that you're still on your way to that eternal punishment you've always deserved.

Temptations are out there all over, particularly from those others who aren't right-wing Christians. Constant vigilance over your personal inherently evil nature is necessary if you don't want to get what you really deserve "without Jesus."

THE WARMTH OF BELIEVING WE'RE WORTHY ONLY OF ABUSE

What kind of country must the US be when the majority of us feel so negative about ourselves that such claims are popularly welcomed? How hurt we must be deep within our psyches that even the so-called "saved" among us still devalue themselves as essentially worthy only of the endless torture they call hell.

Many Americans apparently understand themselves and their fellow humans as really deserving such hell. Opinion polls indicate that anywhere from 54% to 85% of US citizens believe hell exists, another indication that Americans have widely absorbed conservative teachings.

The right-wing doctrine of hell strikes as familiar an emotional cord as the idea that humans are inherently worthless. Hell is a familiar idea because we've experienced our hells on earth.

The doctrine sanctifies the idea that God is a punishing father whom we are supposed to accept as both the paradigm of what love is and as a father who also believes that we deserve unending physical, emotional, and psychological abuse. It's as if we are supposed to define love this way. A loving person, parent, or god would be loving toward us even as they tell us we're evil and deserve brutal, unceasing abuse.

Any human parent who could save their child, no matter what the child did, from far less cruel and inhuman violence than hell represents but allows that child to suffer unendingly and argues that the child deserves such suffering would be arrested for neglect and abuse in any state in the union. Their parenting ability itself would be questioned from all sides including most religious conservatives.

Children who came to believe about their human parents what this idea claims about a heavenly father would be textbook cases in the minds of many therapists for addictive behavior if not deep psychosis. They'd fit the classic example of an abused child. Yet that's just what right-wing religion expects when "children of God" face the Father of all that is.

"There are countless theological explanations for the motives behind God's inscrutable counsels," child development and trauma expert Alice Miller writes in *The Truth Will Set You Free: Overcoming Emotional Blindness and Finding Your True Adult Self,* "but in all too many of them I see a terrorized child trying hard to interpret the mysterious actions of the parents as good and loving, even though the child cannot fathom them — indeed, has no chance of fathoming them."

Such religious and spiritual abuse as found in the right-wing picture of hell, then, appeals because it feels familiar. It's at home in that deep warm place within anyone's subconscious that was prepared to receive it by how they were raised by the adults around them. The doctrine of hell sounds like the nightmare of an abused child who's been told it deserves the violent and shaming punishment a parent dishes out "for their own good."

Much parenting in our culture fits the definition of "poisonous pedagogy" about which Alice Miller writes in books such as *For Your Own Good: Hidden Cruelty in Child-Rearing and the Roots of Violence* and *Thou Shalt Not Be Aware: Society's Betrayal of the Child.*

Right-wing doctrines of human evil and hell are replete with familiar themes found in still dominant conservative parenting. It's this form of parenting on an international level that actually makes violence so common, Miller argues. Yet, fearing the effects of inherently evil children loose on the earth, and consistent with the messages parents had internalized during their own childhoods, such parenting methods are often hidden politely and justified righteously under mottoes such as: "dare to discipline."

One need look no further than the 4th century "father" of this dominant Christian theology of human depravity and innate worthlessness to see a young St. Augustine physically and otherwise abused by his own father and his male teachers. As Princeton University Professor of Pastoral Theology, Donald Capps, shows in *The Child's Song: The Religious Abuse of Children*, Augustine confesses he was a severely beaten small child. Then, after internalizing this message of his own depravity, Augustine writes later about the innate evil of all children's natures. As a father, Augustine rejected his own son as one "born out of sin," and, Capps observes, probably caused his only child's early death.

In circular fashion, once the doctrine of an inherent human evil that deserves eternal punishment is accepted, it reinforces the need for the parental "poisonous pedagogy" that prepares the next generation for embracing the doctrine. "It supports the abuse of children," Capps argues, "by providing theological legitimation for the physical punishment of children, and it more directly abuses children by promoting beliefs and ideas that are inherently tormenting to children."

It's not that every child is physically abused. Yet most grown adults would rather not face the fact that their parents, who were taught to do so by their own parents, used parenting methods that internalized in our citizens a sense of their limited value, shame in who they are, their worthlessness outside of adult acceptance, the fact that they should "Honor their father and mother" no matter what, or the gnawing belief that they're unworthy of respect or of being taken seriously.

This dominant theology appeals to something deep within the child-rearing process, something so accepted that it's often unnoticed or just denied. Passed down from generation to generation by childrearing is the prepared soil for the planting and replanting of the theological teaching of human unworthiness, innate incivility, and "original sin."

Hell is not merely a cosmic picture of physical abuse, nor is it only a projection on the universe of one's personal parenting. Its power also comes from the fact that it touches essentially on the emotional abuse that speaks in eternal abandonment and triggers familiar "abandonment issues" that therapists find rampant in our society.

Fear of abandonment is a persistent and foundational emotion behind all addictions, from alcoholism to sexual addiction, according to experts on addiction. It's the worst fear for a child — worse than physical abuse. It motivates adults into all sorts of addictive behaviors around romance and relationships. Abandonment means the child (and the grown adult child) is unwanted and unworthy of love.

The picture of hell as the place of abandonment that all

humans in themselves deserve could not more vividly touch the inner child's unhealed fears, fears taught to them in thousands of ways from the adults around them.

FEAR AND LOATHING IN AMERICAN SOCIETY

There is more to the emotional effectiveness of hell as fear of abandonment than is evident from looking at messages children inherited from parents and other grown-ups in their early life. Hell also touches on all the culturally installed fears of violence, threats, ridicule, humiliation, isolation, and rejection — the methods our larger society itself uses, I've argued in *Scared Straight: Why It's So Hard to Accept Gay People and Why It's So Hard to Be Human,* to install gender and other roles in us.

Note how the right wing fears changing these personal and societal patterns. That's why it criticizes "over-indulgence" of children, so-called "New Age" affirmations of humanity's innate goodness, beliefs that the Divine is not found outside but within every human being, or anyone who suggests children have something to teach an adult world that's run by leaders who sound like punishing parents. Even the most liberal among us get caught sounding like our punishing parents, particularly when children won't be seen and not heard.

Like Bradshaw, Miller in *For Your Own Good* is blunt: "For some years now, there has been proof that the devastating effects of the traumatization of children take their inevitable toll on society — a fact that we are still forbidden to recognize. This knowledge concerns every one of us and — if disseminated widely enough — should lead to fundamental changes in society; above all, to a halt in the blind escalation of violence."

Too much would have to be admitted, faced, and confessed if our society considered this too seriously. Too much personal pain would need to be felt about our own childhoods. It's easier to just believe that we all deserve hell and seek a fix.

Add to this doctrine right-wing marketing techniques they've picked up from business and the entertainment industry — its effectiveness at convincing people of their innate evil. The Christian right, after all, dominated radio and television from their infancy with radio evangelists, and TV preachers. Today the media seek them out for religious commentary.

Somehow the alternative understandings of religious liberalism regarding human nature were marginalized. Religious liberals were left behind politically as formerly other-worldly conservatives decided to form a Christian Coalition that could turn the US into a theocracy with the religious right-wing in charge.

There was hesitancy on the liberal side of the Christian Church. Maybe it was liberal guilt. Maybe it was the belief that modern life would automatically leave these traditional beliefs behind so that they didn't need to fight the right-wing. Maybe it was their own way not to face the personal feelings that might be raised, feelings that have roots in the childhoods of now liberal adults who were raised by conservative parents. Maybe it was the impression that spreading the word was somehow low-class. Whatever it was, the rise of the religious right politically enforced the broad-based impression that Fundamentalism, including its negative view of the human being, *is* Christianity.

Then, enforce such messages with the speeches and scoldings of dominant political leaders whose solution to problems is not to seek causes but to increase the severity of punishment for offenders. The result: **adults have a desperate need for a fix to provide relief from self-denigrating, self-abusive feelings of their innate evil.**

The high of religious addiction, like all other addictive fixes, protects the addict from facing any destructive feelings that go back to childhood. The right-wing doctrines of an evil human nature unworthy of love and of threats of abandonment in hell resonate with and enforce these feelings, justify them cosmically, and impel believers to seek a fix in the high of addictions. For many, the fix of choice is found in religion.

Most emotional problems that are not of physical origin,

therapists observe, are related to low self-esteem. Feelings of worthlessness, unacceptability, desperate evil within, and incompetence are characteristic of those with negative understandings of themselves.

This has little to do with intelligence. People who are the most gifted often have strong, even overwhelming, feelings of inadequacy.

Low-self esteem is the core issue in addictions. In fact, both addiction and the codependence characteristic of the addict's enablers are rooted in low self-esteem. Essentially through their highs, addictions are meant to counter the feelings that characterize the negative self-image of the addict.

"Low self-esteem," Twerski says, "refers to the negative feelings people have about themselves that are not justified by fact."

Yet, what if the religion you accept as the one that defines what the facts of life are teaches that your low self-esteem is the fact? You really are low. It's like the old quip: "You're not paranoid; everyone really *is* out to get you."

That's the case of conservative Christian religion and its teaching of the sinful condition of humanity that deserves hell. You really, in yourself, deserve to have low self-esteem because, no doubt about it, you are a "wretch." You must find your value outside of yourself.

That's what makes the high of being righteous so addictive. It's a fix, a relief from those feelings about oneself that just can't be written off in right-wing religion as a misunderstanding of one's true worth. You can't dismiss therapeutically these negative feelings as a delusion, distortion, or misunderstanding of your real value. Those feelings are considered the truth, and you're too evil to do anything about it.

You can, however, be "saved" from the eternal, unspeakable punishment you deserve, but in yourself you can never, ever become worthy of anything better than that punishment. Your savior is an Other Being who, unlike you, is truly worthy of respect and heaven.

Add to this the preaching that this only inherently good One experienced the suffering that you really deserve even though he didn't deserve it at all. His suffering underlines and highlights how awful your evil nature and actions are. His suffering was your fault. You ought to be ashamed.

The more that suffering is dwelt upon, the more it's graphically played upon as in Mel Gibson's wildly popular torture film *The Passion of the Christ*, the more ashamed one can feel when they say, "He went through that because of me."

Thus, the need for the fix that numbs the negative feelings, the fix that's taught as true "joy," the fix and the on-going process to renew it on which the addict has become dependent. Any doubt about its truth means facing one's evil self again without the high — that is, facing the feelings of low self-esteem clean and sober.

The words of a member of a right-wing church that calls itself a "Family Worship Center" come close to expressing this need to feel something other than the negative valuation of herself she had accepted. Rejecting "the self" for her was crucial to feeling alive again. It would help her cope with life, whereas others who didn't have the fix, she projected, must be miserable.

"I accepted Christ as my personal savior years ago. I knew then I was totally bad, you know.

"But I've become lukewarm lately. I've always had my ups and downs. God doesn't feel close right now.

"I know I'm the reason for that. My old sin nature is showing through. I've had my doubts. I know it's because I don't pray enough, too.

"You've just got to put down your self and its sin — 'lose your self.' Faith is important. My goal is to feel God's warm arms around me again. Without that, life is pretty miserable. I can't understand how people who don't know Jesus can get by."

CHAPTER FOUR

IT'S ALL GOD'S FAULT

"I've never seen anything like it," the elderly gentleman sitting next to me on the plane broke the silence as he put down his newspaper. He must have noticed that I was reading a book with the title *When Religion Becomes Evil.*

"That Pat Robertson can say anything nutty he wants and people still pay attention to him. They treat him like he has something valuable to contribute to society. I bet they're still sending him bundles of cash, too. I just don't get people sometimes."

What my seat-mate was struggling to figure out was why one of America's most popular televangelists could still be popular after calling for assassinations of world figures, agreeing that terrorist attacks on the US and severe storms were from God to punish the televangelist's usual scapegoats, and now asserting that God was punishing an Israeli prime minister with a stroke and its complications.

"I think we're seeing the characteristics of addictive religion," I tried to explain — as best as I can remember and not sure that I fully made my point. "These are 'true believers' who've bet their life on Robertson's ideas and personality. They personally need to believe what he says to feel good about themselves and not feel as if they've been fools to trust him.

"They'll hang in there, make excuses for him, ignore his actual words, forgive him again and again, and keep giving money. They *can't* let go. If they do, they'll feel as if they're at sea again. They'd have to face things they don't want to face."

"I just don't get it," he repeated. "People don't make sense."

To those outside the addiction, believers who are addicted to religion don't make sense. They don't seem to think logically. That's not surprising, because no addictive thinking makes sense to those outside it.

As Twerski puts it: "Although addictive thinkers turn logic around, they are absolutely convinced that their logic is valid. They not only resist rational arguments to the contrary, but also they cannot understand why others do not see the 'obvious.'"

Looking for the logic in the thinking of addicts is a waste of time. The goal of all addictive thinking and acting, after all, is to do what it takes to keep the good feelings going and get the next high. It's to prevent the addicted from being left to deal with what they see as a Reality out to get them and with their own sinful selves.

It's crucial to understand the depth of emotions the righteous high is meant to prevent the addict from feeling. So, let me emphasize that the key to addictive religion is that it will do anything not to feel the negative view of human beings it also promotes and its believers have internalized.

In fact, since right-wing religion itself promotes that negative, abusive view of human beings, its very promotion enforces the need for a fix. Take away the teaching of human depravity, its influence throughout society, and all of the old, continually failing responses that assume the teaching is true, and addictive religion would lose its true believers.

THE USING BEHAVIORS OF ADDICTIVE RELIGION

The activities of addictive religion function as what recovery groups call "using behaviors." These behaviors are meant to produce, enforce, and replicate the "high." Since addictions require ever more intense highs to keep the feelings of worthlessness at bay, there is an incredibly powerful incentive to seek those new and more intense religious highs by replicating using behaviors.

People caught up in addictive religion, like those in any addiction, didn't set out to be addicted. They set out to feel better. They really wanted "good news" — which is, after all, what the word "gospel" promises. By the time they're addicted, though, the religious behaviors seem so normal and the corresponding thinking so sensible to the addicts that they seldom question these behaviors.

In fact, they're often taught not to question them. If someone within addictive religion were to question the behaviors of the religion in any meaningful way, there would be immediate negative responses that enforce the sense that the addictive beliefs and behaviors are normal.

Appearing to rebel, successful questioners learn, will pit the powerful united church and its allies against them. Institutional and community responses are likely to include threats of separation, humiliation, rejection, negative consequences in this life, and, of course, eternal punishments.

Actually, believers should have already internalized a set of feelings about themselves as well. So, questioning and doubt beyond the allowable limits raises both external and internalized messages that it's the addict's evil nature that is causing the questioning, not the addiction.

The evolution of the righteousness high has taken a major turn in the United States with the political ascendancy of the religious-become-political right-wing of Christianity. What had called itself Fundamentalism, Conservative Evangelicalism, Biblical literalists, and even "the truly saved" in the last decades took a new tact that would produce more intense highs.

Prior to the rise of these religio-political aspirations, though, huddling together in congregations seemed enough for producing and renewing this high. In their meetings and services they could be together with those who felt the same misery, heard that there was nothing they could do to be "saved," and shared the high of righteousness.

In spite of what might have been better intentions, most of

these church meetings didn't function for their members like recovery groups, providing support to overcome the addiction and affirm the value of each human being. These church services were more like opium dens. They consisted of "using behaviors," which they promoted, that functioned to further internalize the addiction by altering the users' moods.

Audio-visual technological developments, contemporary music, and high-tech electronics were enlisted to heighten the experience. Church services often were meant to produce emotional responses on the level of professional sporting events, bars, and dance clubs, though with a different set of addictive substances. One could hear preachers ask why people didn't demonstrate that they were "fans for the Lord" as enthusiastically as they were for their NFL teams.

Addiction recovery groups begin with the problem of the addiction, focus on honestly telling the stories of the addiction without judgment, and provide a community that doesn't teach that its members are any better than everyone outside the meeting. Recovery groups attract by word of mouth, not through the latest business and media advertising techniques. Attendees believe that they are in recovery. Addiction specialists also recognize that the addict's thinking is ultimately based upon low self-esteem and shame.

Church attendees quickly learned not to be honest about their difficulties, worries, fears, lapses, and questions when in church gatherings. Pat answers were dolled out and repeated over and over again that, instead of convincing attendees they were being heard, basically preached that problems were caused by their own lack of religious practices — prayer, Bible reading, regular attendance at church services and other church meetings, tithing, self-denial, and witnessing.

Practicing these using behaviors could renew the high the believer sought again. Even more of the addiction would save them from lingering doubts and insecurities. Religious retreats and evangelistic meetings were events meant to revive even more intense highs.

Any complaints they had were to be blamed on lack of faith and lack of using. Taken too far, deviation meant that the threat of demonic possession or eternal damnation also loomed ahead for an "unbeliever." It may even mean they have committed "the unpardonable sin," a vague sword of Damocles that can hang over anyone because of the inability of anyone to explain convincingly and with clarity what the New Testament meant when it made the threat.

The high, being "happy in the Lord," is an important symptom to show the others. To admit that it's not working or unsuccessful is to admit personal failure. One can even begin to feel that they're walking on eggshells around other religious addicts. You learn what not to say and how to cover your "failures in the walk."

"They talked about the importance of honesty and sharing," a young woman said. "They also talked about being open. But I soon learned that there were certain things you couldn't talk about, things you couldn't question. There was a real gap between the minister preaching he was saved by grace like the rest of us, and anybody actually talking about what was really going on in their life. You just couldn't admit you weren't getting more Christ-like every day."

The more one attends the meetings, hears the sermons, devours the literature, listens to the radio and TV programs, and learns the clearly accepted form of behaviors such as prayer, the more one learns the vocabulary. Addictive religion has a jargon that seems meaningful inside the addiction but sounds strange, hokey, quaint, and jingoistic to those outside it.

Responding with these insider phrases often becomes a final answer to a problem, even if these answers are merely thought-terminating clichés. Accepting the cliché at face value feels as if one has gotten an answer. If not, one soon learns not to question the cliché.

One is reminded of the old story about the long-term prison inmates who had told each other the same jokes for so many years that they only had to mention the number they'd given each joke to get a laugh.

"I forgot what number 16 was," one newcomer said. The rest looked at him as if he had broken some rule, but no one else could remember. They just knew it was really funny.

Thus, just saying: "The Bible says," or "The Ten Commandments forbid," or "It's the inspired word," ends thinking. Responses can be intimidating: "Are you questioning God's Word?" "Are you praying regularly?" "Whose opinion should we accept, yours or God's?" One doesn't question.

I remember a devout, highly regarded elderly woman, whose church called her a "prayer-warrior," praying at a midweek "prayer meeting:" "As Thou hast said, where there's a will there's a way." Now, as far as I know, "Thou" didn't say that, unless he is Ben Franklin in *Poor Richard's Almanac.*

"Please, lead us to the throne of grace" is definitely more religious than "Please pray." And the archaic language of the King James Bible with its "thou" and "ye" contributes to the thought-numbing nature of the experience. It gives the language an authority that the current everyday speech of plain human beings just doesn't have.

SHAME AND GUILT AND THE ADDICT'S FIX

Addictive religious communities make little practical distinction between guilt and shame. In fact, the easiest way to get people to want to be "saved" from the evil within them was to play on shame.

Whereas guilt is the belief that a person has done something wrong, shame is the feeling that the person themselves is wrong. Shame then goes still further, for it convinces someone that they are shamed in the sight of others. Shame encourages someone to cover their shame because they feel as if they are, or could be, exposed to the humiliating, judgmental sight of others.

The story of Adam and Eve tells of a shame in their nakedness before their Maker's gaze, which they cover with fig leaves. Children were taught early that the Heavenly Father was looking down upon their every move and seeing all the bad things they were doing.

Most often among right-wing Christians the object of this shaming was sexuality. It was easy to do in a society in which sexual activity was to be hidden from sight and discussion.

Any sex education at all within these churches was primitive, fear-based, and shame-based, after all. They would be the last institutions to embrace modern, scientific sexual research. Most still refuse to do so, fearing that it will set loose some repressed sexual fantasies — though it's always the "sinful" sexual activity of someone else that's condemned publicly, especially by clergy who'll get caught with their own sexual addictions.

The message drilled into prospective clergy was: just don't do it until you're in a heterosexual marriage. Add shame to the mix and the jist was often: "Sex is dirty. Save it for the one you love."

Alfred Kinsey's early sexual research discoveries were too much of a threat — and still are for most. For Roman Catholic clergy the official message was: "Just don't do it at all; it's only meant for reproduction. Now, go and counsel others."

Addictive religion's preachers dealt the high that would compensate for the shame. They did nothing to make people feel as if they were, or could in themselves become, worthwhile. Preachers and theologians instead reinforced their listeners' negative self-concepts and their inability to take responsibility to improve themselves. No one could do anything in themselves to be acceptable. Everything they'd do to try should be seen as anti-God.

In fact, these religious leaders convinced their flocks that they were so evil that they shouldn't trust their own intuitions, thoughts, interpretations, or any positive feelings they might have about themselves. Trusting yourself was put down as "New Age Religion."

As the self-help movement became popular, there were

attempts to incorporate its appeal in the religion. Self-help type books began to appear. The style was easy to incorporate, but the core message still remained that there was nothing they could do in themselves to heal the shame in the eyes of the only One who really counted.

They could only be acceptable because another Being really, really, really would accept them in spite of their evil. Only when people accepted that notion, was it okay to feel "joy." That should be enough for a high.

They could also feel as if the "lost," people out there, were the ones with problems, not them. Those out there were "getting away with" sins of all sorts, whereas true believers like them have their evil nature under control. Projection of their own view of themselves, which was much like self-hatred, on others could help relieve negative feelings about themselves.

There were rules, "laws" like "The Ten Commandments," that they should follow, and others should too. Obsessing over obedience to such rules could also redirect mental energy away from other thoughts and emotions. Becoming exemplary models of religious rules offered safety and assurance that one can be perfect in spite of feelings otherwise.

Enforcing the rules on others projected their attention outward away from inner issues. At times it looked as it the more legalistic of church leaders were the most upset by what they felt others were getting away with. One is reminded of the old definition of a Puritan — someone who is afraid that somehow, someway, somewhere, at some time, someone might be having fun.

Right-wing believers would lap up "prophecy." There would often be divisive debates over how to interpret the highly elaborate beliefs about the end time that they constructed by piecing together diverse passages from the Bible.

Yet, what was common to all of their versions of the future was that all of them assured these true believers that though there were satanic forces out to destroy them, they'd come out winners in the end. Those who didn't participate in their addiction would be proven wrong by being "Left Behind."

Hal Lindsey's 1970 bestseller, *The Late, Great Planet Earth*, about the coming tribulation of non-believers and vindication of right-wing Christians became the top selling non-fiction book of the 1970s. It popularly expressed the guarantee of a victory over the world's evil that would vindicate the commitment right-wing religion demands.

THE RELIGIOUS ADDICT'S FLIGHT FROM RESPONSIBILITY

Every idea that was acceptable to right-wing Christianity, every doctrine, every ritual had to be traced to God. Fights would break out, separating churches, over whether minute details were true to "God's Word."

Once, for example, they took their stand for righteousness against the other "so-called Christians" by defending the idea that the only true baptism is by full immersion as opposed to sprinkling or pouring, then they went on to argue over whether it is God's will that they baptize someone three times forward or once backward. Next the argument was: should the baptizer who baptizes someone by dunking in the approved manner say "In the name of the Father, Son, and Holy Ghost" or "In the name of Jesus."

There was no room to justify a thought, idea, belief, or practice on the basis of someone's logical thinking, intuitions, or emotions. The believer's own thoughts are suspect, for they are likely to arise out of their depraved mind. You can't trust yourself and your thoughts. They might even be demonic.

Thus, addictive religion promotes, enforces, and relies upon a key characteristic of addictive thinking and acting. **Addicts do not take responsibility for their addictive thinking and acting. They blame the addiction, others, or the Universe for what they think and do with the addiction.**

There is certainly much talk within right-wing religion about the importance of each individual making a personal decision of faith. One cannot be "saved" on the basis of someone else's faith. Just as the alcoholic is responsible for drinking, the believer takes responsibility for being a part of the religious community.

But once immersed in the addiction, every thought that's believed to be true is Someone Else's fault. Personal responsibility for one's religious beliefs and activities becomes absent when they are considered true beliefs.

Religious addiction blames God for its beliefs and activities, not the individual human beings who hold the beliefs and perform the actions. Blaming God eliminates personal responsibility for the addiction and its results. It frees the religious addicts from having to wonder if their ideas or actions are misunderstandings, or even wrong.

If God, or the Bible, or tradition, or the Church is the cause of a belief, then I am not responsible for it and its consequences.

I am not responsible for how it affects and even hurts others or leaves others out.

I don't have to worry about the fact that others object to me foisting my religious views on them because I'm just passing on God's Truth for them, not my own opinion.

I'm not responsible for its truth at all. I don't have to think too deeply about why it's true.

I'm not responsible for explaining, proving, or justifying the ideas. I can even take pride in the fact that I have "simple faith."

I don't even have to worry about researching personally about other ways to understand reality — they're wrong. After all, my beliefs aren't mine. They're God's ideas and God isn't wrong.

I don't have to question my motives or reasons for embracing these doctrines instead of other doctrines that disagree with them. I don't have to question whether I believe them because they fit with my fears about people, or my family upbringing.

It's not because of who will like me for believing this. It's not because it will solve some inner issues about need-ing to ensure my parents' love.

It's not my fault, bad idea, poor interpretation, or misun-derstanding. It's what God says.

It's not my need to protect what I treasure — my financ-es, my family, my status, my manhood or womanhood, or my image of myself.

Believing this has nothing to do with my fears in life. It's not my relief at not having personally, without hiding behind someone else's authority, to challenge society's larger values and institutions.

It's not because it justifies a prejudice I have about "other" people who are not like me.

It's not because it's a doctrine that protects my "stash."

It's not because it's a way to wash my hands of the abuse that this belief or practice heaps on other people.

It's not because it means I now don't have to feel respon-sible for how others feel about me because I believe it.

None of this is my fault. It's because God says so.

How often do we see this in action? "I wouldn't be against gay people," they say. "But the Bible is. So, I have to be."

What they are saying is that it has nothing to do with their, or cultural, prejudices that cause them to interpret the Bible that way. "I'm innocent. I'm a nice person. It's the Bible's fault." Or, really, "It's God's fault. He is to blame. He's the one who doesn't like them."

A common way to deny personal responsibility so as to blame God and look as if it's not the believer's own problem is to say: "I love the sinner, but I hate the sin," a phrase never found in the Bible. Again, the religious addict is saying, it's God and his teachings; it's not me. I'm for everyone. "Me, I'm innocent of any consequences."

When people blame God, then their abuse is not their abuse. God is the abuser. They're the innocent bystander. So, they can respond as if they are victims: "please don't kill the messenger."

To say instead: "This is how I interpret this passage of the Bible" or "This is how I understand this" is to take personal responsibility for one's beliefs and to be willing to face their consequences. It's to use what counselors call "I" messages.

But one has then opened oneself to the thought that there might be other interpretations and understandings — which there usually are. That opening would push each person to take responsibility for looking at themselves and asking why the understanding they have accepted is the one they should believe and promote, and why others should also accept it.

To say, "It's what God says," is to act like alcoholics who blame everyone but themselves for their drinking and its consequences. "I'm the nice guy. It's God who is the rat."

In the extreme, leaders of addictive religion remove themselves totally from responsibility. They begin to speak directly for God. "God told me." "God put this message on my heart." "I heard the Lord say." "God called me to tell you...." These are common claims from right-wing preachers and televangelists, the dealers of addictive religion.

Once people accept that God Himself is behind their statements, the conversation is stopped. The leader's claim of not being responsible prevents questioning and preserves the authority of their ideas and, thus, their status.

THE NEED FOR THEIR RELIGION TO BE RIGHT

Once someone is convinced of this schema, the need not to question this theology or those who teach it feels like self-preservation. Since right-wing Christians often come to identify their salvation with the televangelists and preachers who deliver it, trust in these leaders no matter what they do becomes more desperate.

No matter what these leaders do, the addicted quickly forgive their leaders, expecting them to get back on the wagon. The leaders' obsessive negative judgments about sins, in which we later might catch them engaged, even leaders acting out sexually after much preaching against it, do not cause the addicted to see hypocrisy or question what they've heard.

The religion must be right and I must seek to affirm its truth against all doubt and the threats from outside that might cause me to question the theology of a God who would, and should, be angry with me, except for the fact that he substituted someone else for punishment.

Addicted ones come to the position where they can't question. All this must be overlooked to maintain the addiction. Otherwise, there are too many issues to face.

What would the believer believe or do instead? How would a believer feel to be so thoroughly duped about something upon which they have bet their life? What then would be the solution to their inherent evil natures? That people still do leave potentially addictive religion is a testimony to the human capacity of will and courage.

Obsession with getting one's theology absolutely right, crossing all those doctrinal "t's" and dotting all those abstract "i's," can become central. Making sure that people's theology is straight takes precedence over all else that makes up human experience and human relationships.

Right-wing religion is highly head-driven and disembodied. One can listen to the theological arguments of fifty years ago, leave the discussion for decades, and return to find the same arguments in progress.

By US cultural standards this emphasis on doctrinal correctness over emotional and physical connection is dominated by prevailing standards of patterned masculinity. Men are conditioned in our culture to be out of touch with their bodies and emotions, and caught up in their minds. In our culture, it's supposed to be women, not real men, who are emotional to the point of being unable to control their emotions. Men are only supposed to experience from the neck up and the waist down, nothing heart-centered.

Rigid theological correctness, getting caught up in disputes over theological intricacies, and demanding theological rigidity, keep one in one's head and away from emotions and feelings of inadequacy and fears of the effeminateness of emotions. One might start feeling how others feel when addicts judge them for their non-abusive beliefs.

Even where religious experience is expected in right-wing religion, it's controlled by doctrine. One must "test the spirits" by solid, approved, correct theology.

The centrality of the correct, approved thinking to right-wing religion also maintains a sense of control over an otherwise threatening, ambiguous world. This need to feel as if one is in, and under, control is a key characteristic of addictive thinking.

The language of addictive religion may speak of a Divine Controller who is supposed to ensure that all that appears to happen is really under His watchful eye and in His hand. No matter how out of control things may appear to be, that belief itself functions to assure the addict that everything is really, really in control. There will be no surprises or new happenings that can raise the fear that things are not really under anyone's control.

Tightly controlling religious beliefs by fixing them in stone and defending them is therefore necessary. Correct, precise, settled, nonevolving beliefs about God and Divine activity must be maintained. Deviations must be prevented or the universe feels threatening.

The Bible's "apparent" diversity must be interpreted through schemes that give the impression that its view of the Divine is unchanging. At the same time, this process of interpretation must be viewed not as the problem of contemporary students interpreting an ancient document but as a rehashing of eternal Truth.

New information cannot be tolerated because it could be a threat. It must be controlled by concealing or manipulating it. Medicine, science, and non-dogmatic education require complexity. They are therefore suspect and must be controlled.

This can be accomplished by separating themselves from any knowledge that addicted one's fear, by removing children from public schools, and by doing all one can to withhold threatening knowledge and even its discussion from the general population.

Notice how the right-wing works to limit public discussion. It doesn't even want information about recognition of the loving relationships of gay people, women's reproductive choice, or evolution available to people unless it can control it.

Being in intellectual control ensures that what will arise will not threaten the high of righteousness. Right thinking suppresses the possibility of some "irrational," even uncontrollable, emotions from surfacing. Emotions are assumed to be sinfully unreliable. So they are ignored or suppressed.

Revelation itself must be controlled. So, it's either consigned to the past (not available to current believers) or restricted to a few approved leaders. For right-wing Protestants, there is no revelation outside the Bible. The Bible must be the "closed canon" of God's Word to human beings, containing all that is "sufficient for salvation" and most anything else.

For some conservatives though, such as the Southern Baptists, the right-wing charismatic movement with its speaking in tongues posed a threat because people might claim a personal revelation directly from God that was not "Biblical." Strict controls on what "the Spirit said" were crucial to keep every idea subordinate to the closed canon of acceptable revelation.

EITHER FOR US OR AGAINST US

An addictive approach to reality is characterized by dualistic thinking not subtlety and nuance. Ambiguity of many kinds (sexual, moral, spiritual, gender) is confusing and unsettling. It might cause us to question the neat, settled, categories of our upbringings.

Schaef in *When Society Becomes an Addict* points out that dualistic thinking has an easy appeal. Most of us, she notes, were educated in dualistic thinking in order to oversimplify a complex world and give us a feeling that the world is not as complex as it appears. "When we think we can break something that has complex facets into two clear dimensions," Schaef observes, "it feeds our illusion of control."

For the addicted, however, ambiguity becomes frightening. There can be no shades of gray. Things must be either good or evil, black or white, right or wrong. You are either saved or a sinner, god-like or demonic, perfect or worthless, for us or against us.

Either/or thinking also erects boundaries that severely limit someone's view of life. It prevents a person who sees the world dualistically from being able to consider alternatives to the two limited alternatives.

"In dualistic thinking," Schaef cautions, "if we state that something is *right*, then the assumption is that the opposite is *wrong*. The world is perceived as pairs of opposites. There is no recognition that both 'opposites' can be right, or that there may be other alternatives besides the two. The very process of dualism prevents us from generating or considering alternatives."

Dualistic, either/or thinking, Booth notes, "is one of the predominant symptoms of addictive religion." It's another tool that helps religious addicts maintain a sense of control over a world they otherwise would find threatening. Shades of gray confuse and threaten right-wing addictive religion.

Things must feel settled and unchanging. Every issue must fit into a neat and tidy resolution. Being confronted by the need to choose the lesser of two evils or the greater of two goods can feel as if there are no correct choices.

So, leaders who market their positions with black-or-white answers function as the saviors of religious addicts. They save them from the fear that there aren't any definite answers and that no one is really in control. Thus, the phrase "situation ethics" became a mind-numbing right-wing catchphrase to put down non-dualistic ethical thinking by more liberal Christian thinkers and anyone else.

All of this ultimately denies personal responsibility for the belief claims right-wing religion preaches. It makes their religious and moral claims less personal and more abstract. Abstracting away from one's own experience and into the mind is an effective method to respond to challenges.

At other times one can also hear the anger that religious addicts express when their beliefs are challenged in a way that they feel threatens them. Booth advises: "People who are spiritually healthy will not react with fear and anger to questions about their beliefs and practices."

Not being responsible for one's own beliefs and actions by blaming God, protecting oneself from the threat of emotions one does not want to feel or even acknowledge, ignoring the hypocrisy of the dealers of addictive religion, thinking of the victims of addictive religion impersonally, and controlling a threatening world by dualistic thinking are ways not to face oneself and take responsibility for one's beliefs and actions. These are characteristics of addictive thinking.

Their goal is to restore and renew the high of righteousness. As in all addictions, as the addicts became more addicted, the fix becomes more desperate. Services were the gathering together of addicts for another drink, another line.

But addictions are progressive and higher fixes are required. So where would those addicted to religion go next to get the even heavier doses that would alter the moods that could threaten their high?

CHAPTER FIVE

NOT SO STRANGE BEDFELLOWS —
SEXUAL AND RELIGIOUS ADDICTION

• A popular televangelist is caught in a motel with a known prostitute.

• Hundreds of Roman Catholic priests are accused and found guilty of sexual activity with their young male and female parishioners.

• Settlements with those who feel sexually abused by priests are in the tens of millions of dollars. Dioceses file for bankruptcy.

• A pastor is asked to resign from a local church because he has had an affair with a member's wife.

• A police prostitution sting picks up a prominent leader of a suburban megachurch.

• A Tulsa Southern Baptist pastor and member of the denomination's executive committee who is outspoken against homosexuality is arrested in another city for, and admits, soliciting a male undercover cop.

• The President of the National Association of Evangelicals and pastor of a 14,000-member Colorado Springs church who bragged about the frequency of Evangelicals having sex but railed regularly against homosexuality is forced to step down after admitting his relationship with a Denver male hustler.

Stories of the sexual exploits of ministers who are known to rail against the sexuality that the stories expose are notorious and common. We've come to expect more to appear monthly. Religious leaders who are the most outspoken for centering their messages on condemning the sexuality of others provide routine public examples of the old Biblical admonition to "Judge not, lest ye be judged."

Inducing guilt and shame by focusing one's preaching on people's sex lives is a historically proven tactic in many religious traditions, and in conservative Christianity in particular. Preaching that the fires of hell are burning to torment anyone obsessed by sexual thoughts is a surefire message to drive adolescents and others to church altars in a culture that constantly uses sex to promote consumption.

Obsession with religion and sex seem to go hand in hand. Religious addiction and sexual addiction are common bedfellows and have many similarities.

This connection doesn't surprise specialists who study both addictions. Leo Booth in *When God is a Drug* cites numerous examples of how, "there is such a great correlation between sexual abuse and religious addiction and abuse."

The existence of multiple addictions in an addict has become a common expectation for addiction counselors. Experts point out that addictions are more often multiple than not. A person with one usually has at least one other.

"It may be that one of the greatest, unacknowledged contributors to recidivism in alcoholism," sexual addiction specialist Patrick Carnes writes in his pioneering *Out of the Shadows: Understanding Sexual Addiction*, "is the failure of treatment programs to treat multiple addictions."

The Christian Church's on-going obsession with sex and sexuality, the centrality it has put on controlling and forbidding sexuality in its message of sinfulness, is a suspicious sign that religious addiction and sexual addiction have been regularly re-enforcing each other. In the middle of ethical challenges as large as war, suffering, diseases, failing relationships, and poverty, right-wing religion is obsessed with controlling sexuality, not just its own but everyone's worldwide.

Preaching that's based on fears of unbridled sexual

expression has become a money raiser. One need only mouth the phrase "The Gay Agenda" in right-wing churches to raise the specter of fear within these churches that all hell is about to break loose destroying their marriages, families, children, lives, religious institutions, societies, and planet.

The Roots of Sexual Addiction for Religious Addicts

To say that obsession with sexuality and its control has been one of the major interests of the dominant institutions of many religions, and certainly much of Christianity from the time of the Apostle Paul until the present, is hardly a revelation. An analysis of Paul's concern with controlling sexuality has caused some scholars to conclude that his sexual urges, and possibly his own homosexuality, was what he referred to when he wrote to the Church in Corinth of his persistent "thorn in the flesh," which God had refused to remove.

An abundance of historical scholarship has analyzed the topic and even concluded that historically Christian leaders have been characterized by an eroto-phobia, fear of the erotic itself. The erotic, after all, is difficult to control.

The dominant strand of theology in the Church can be traced back through the fourth century theologian Augustine of Hippo, who was probably the most influential thinker in all of Christian history. Augustine's negative theories of human nature and the relationship of human depravity to sexuality set the tone for most later Roman Catholic and Protestant thinking. He popularized the proclamation that sin was inherited from parents and, therefore, actually passed down to the next generation by means of sexual intercourse.

It became vitally important, therefore, that Christians believe that Jesus was an exception to this line of sexual contagiousness and, thus, to defend the dogma of his virgin birth. Eventually Roman Catholic theology would have to preserve Jesus' mother Mary from the same sin/sex fate, and so embraced the idea that she was not only a "perpetual virgin," but "conceived without sin" through the dogma of the Immaculate Conception.

The ideas of Augustine, this Father of Christian theology, made political sense for the formation of a religion that could ensure loyalty to the Roman Empire. The new political situation under the "Christian" government of Emperor Constantine and later Christian emperors required the allegiance of Christians, who before Constantine had been persecuted by the Roman government.

The adoption of Augustine's thought provided a standardized theology that enabled Rome to politically unite its citizens. In addition, it propagated a religious reason why citizens should conform to the dominant institutions of Rome — all humans are inherently evil and therefore in need of control by a government claiming to be ordained by God and doing God's work.

"Traditional declarations of human freedom, forged by martyrs defying the emperor as the anti-Christ incarnate," writes historian Elaine Pagels in *Adam, Eve, and the Serpent*, "no longer fit the situation of Christians who found themselves, under Constantine and his Christian successors, the emperor's 'brothers and sisters in Christ.'"

It's clear from Augustine's own writings that his theological theories about sin and sex — those ideas that would become central to right-wing Christianity today — arose out of his personal problems with his sexuality. Augustine turned to religion, and developed out of his confessed powerlessness to control his sex life a form of Christian thought with its view of an inherently evil human nature that would become mainstream.

In his *Confessions* Augustine spoke of what contemporary sexual addiction specialists would call his personal sexual addiction. This autobiography's later self-evaluation of his sexual life is replete with classic confessions of a sexual addict who feels powerless over his addiction.

In Carne's analysis, Augustine is a clear example of a sexual addict who begins by acting out his addiction but then switches to sexual anorexia. He becomes what Alcoholics

Anonymous calls a "dry drunk." His on-going fear of his sexuality and its threat to overpower him maintains his obsession with and condemnation of sex throughout his life and writings.

In *Sexual Anorexia*, Carnes writes: "Many of the early leaders of the Christian church appear to be operating in that mode. St. Augustine, for example, in his *Confessions* describes a period of sexual acting out in his life and then argues for a life of temperance and abstinence. In addition to reflecting the culture in which he lived and wrote, Augustine's story is an example of the addictive switch."

To sample some of Augustine's own words about his sexual addiction: "My invisible enemy trod me down and seduced me because I was easy to be seduced." At the age of sixteen, he writes, "the madness of raging lust exercised its supreme dominion over me." Visiting prostitutes and even fathering a child as a teenager by a concubine proceeded, he says, out of "slavery" to "the habit of satisfying an insatiable lust" that he was afraid ultimately to live without. "I drew my shackles along with me, terrified to have them knocked off." Even a friend, he says, was "amazed at my enslavement" to sex.

As Carnes observes about sexual addicts who have made the anorexic switch that Augustine later made, what remains afterward is: "an unrelenting obsession with and fear of their sexuality, which is reinforced by the tremendous damage caused by their previous sexual behavior. It is almost as if they have been so traumatized by what they have done that sex in any guise becomes the abuser, the enemy."

Augustine's remorse in his *Confessions*, which were written after his switch to a sexually anorexic stance, reflects all of this including his trauma over what he had done before. When he converted to Christian religion and switched the acting out of his sexual addiction to sexual anorexia, he projected his own addiction on every human being, even those who claimed to be chaste.

"What man is there," Augustine writes, "who, being aware

of his own weakness, dares so much as to attribute his chastity and innocence to his own virtue?" His claim was that no one was capable of controlling such lust because all people are too evil. And this inability, rooted in the sinful self that everyone inherits from as far back as Adam, is transmitted through nothing less than the very sexual act that conceives everyone, an act about which he continued to be obsessed.

Even in his more theoretical book, *City of God,* written during his later celibacy, sexuality's uncontrollable power over all humans remained his central concern: "At times, the urge intrudes uninvited; at other times, it deserts the panting lover, and, although desire blazes in the mind, the body is frigid. In this strange way, desire refuses service, not only to the will to procreate, but also to the desire of wantonness; and though for the most part, it solidly opposes the mind's command, at other times it is divided against itself, and, having aroused the mind, it fails to arouse the body."

A life-long obsession with sex, continuing feelings of powerlessness over the addiction, a movement from acting out sexual addiction to an obsession with sexual abstinence and the sinfulness of sex, either/or thinking, projection of his addiction on everyone else, a self-concept based on his own feelings of depravity evidenced by his sexual powerlessness, and an inability to control himself — these are the marks of Augustine's sexual addiction.

Augustinian theology would provide the groundwork for many others for their addictive thinking about sex as well as Christian religious doctrines. With powerful, influential leaders and institutions enforcing and justifying all of this, the ideas of human sinfulness and sexuality became inescapable.

As Augustine's ideas came to dominate orthodoxy in Christian institutions, these institutions too would bear the marks of sexual addiction. Obsession with control of their sexuality would affect their thinking. The all-male Church leaders would project their obsession with sex away from themselves by attempting to control pagan's, women's, non-

Christian's and homosexual's sexuality. Those outside the Church — Jews, Muslims, and others — would be portrayed as evil by accusing them of all sorts of out-of-control sexual activity that Church leadership portrayed as sin, perversion, excess, and lawlessness.

Roman Catholic historian Uta Ranke-Heinemann exhaustively documented what she labels the history of "sexual pessimism" on the part of the Church in her disturbingly candid history, *Eunuchs for the Kingdom of Heaven: Women, Sexuality and the Catholic Church.* Augustine, she concludes is "the man who fused Christianity with hatred of sex and pleasure in a systematic unity."

"Augustine was the great creator of the Christian image of God, the world, and humanity that is still widely accepted today. He took the contempt for sex that saturates the works of the Church Fathers, both before him and in his own day, and to it he added a new factor: A personal and theological sexual anxiety."

THE PREVALENCE OF SEXUAL ADDICTION

All the while, again and again down through history, the addiction would come to public light when clergy and other leaders known for their outspoken negativity toward sexual activity would be found to have illicit affairs, polygamous sexual relationships, and the forbidden sexual practices leaders were blaming on others.

"The irony is that these people were motivated largely by feelings of spiritual inadequacy and unworthiness – much like our contemporary anorexics," Carnes observes in *Sexual Anorexia.* "The result was, not surprisingly, torturous obsession — and a fair amount of sexual acting out. Monks commonly sexually abused women and boys sent for spiritual care (bingeing). In fact, an unmarried pregnant woman who did not want to name the father could falsely accuse a monk of paternity — and be believed."

It's only within the last twenty years that addiction specialists and therapists have begun to identify the existence and prevalence of sexual addiction. Early claims of sexual addiction brought humor more than understanding.

Males in particular would identify with the apparently out-of-control sexual struggles Augustine talked about in his *Confessions*. Enforced by a sex-obsessed media and consumer culture, and by moral and religious leaders who assumed that struggling with chastity and celibacy was normal, they believed that difficulties with sex, called "lust," were normal for men, and set up patriarchal regulations to control the "lust" they feared women embodied.

The dominant attitude of the Church toward sex would confirm that a hard-to-control sexual lust is essential to humanity's depraved condition. So, when the letter to the Hebrews in the New Testament spoke of Jesus as "in all points tempted like as we are, yet without sin," the first thing that would need denial was Jesus' sexuality.

Social scientists note that this acceptance of the idea of the almost uncontrollable "power of sexuality" is partly because sexual addiction is built into our societal institutions, our advertising, our religious institutions, and our very belief about what "normal" or "natural" sexuality is supposed to be. Instead though, the reality is better expressed by the title of sexologist Leonore Tiefer's book, *Sex Is Not a Natural Act*. What is considered normal or natural is actually defined by the culture in which someone grows up and, therefore has varied substantially around the world.

By the end of the twentieth century, the reality and problem of sexual addiction was widely diagnosed. Whole chapters devoted to the topic are now a part of basic medical textbooks. A National Council on Sexual Addiction and Compulsivity publishes a medical journal dedicated to the problem. The existence of Sexual Compulsives Anonymous or groups with similar names indicates that sexual addiction has been recognized worldwide.

Rather than being an isolated phenomenon, sexual addiction, Anne Wilson Schaef, points out in her *Escape from*

Intimacy: Untangling the "Love" Addictions, "is of epidemic proportions in this society and is integrated into the addictiveness of the society as a whole. No treatment of sexual addiction can be complete unless it explores the role of the society and the institutions of the society."

Schaef claims that sexual addiction is one of the addictions most deeply woven into our society as "normal." Clearly it's reflected in the conservative religion that becomes addictive.

THE CHURCH'S DENIAL AND COVER-UP OF SEXUAL ADDICTION

When, for example, the evidence of sexual addiction broke into the news in terms of hundreds of Roman Catholic priests abusing young male parishioners, the Roman Catholic Church didn't examine its institutional obsession. Instead, it did nothing less than any large, multi-national business organization would have done in reaction to a scandal.

This bothers people who expect more from religious institutions than they do from other international bureaucracies such as Enron, Tyco, WorldCom, and Global Crossing, even those who argue that a church should be run like a business. Yet, as priests were accused of sexual abuse and pedophilia, the Church's immediate and routine response was not to question itself, its teachings and culture, but rather cover-up and denial.

The larger an organization, the farther away from the scene of the crimes its top-level executives can "transfer" managers. The Church has more branch office opportunities for hiding employees all around the world. So, priests were passed around the organization when threats of scandal arose.

What challenged this self-protecting pattern was what often brings meaningful, radical change — the persistent intervention of common folk who would no longer make excuses for, and enable, the institution. They were tired of being a part of the cover-up because the price they were paying for protecting the institution was their own emotional well-being. To quote civil rights activist Fannie Lou Hammer, they were "sick and tired of being sick and tired."

Putting on a good face (public relations) was necessary for the Church in denial. To protect its reputation, the organization then tried to settle with the victims. It didn't want questions raised about whether something systemic was going on, whether its very structure, values, thinking about sex, processes, and leadership were really at fault.

Then it argued that the exposed sexual abusers were isolated cases. They were just "rotten apples" while the barrel itself was clean and sober. Meanwhile the number of sexual abuse accusations continued to rise into the thousands.

Finally, the unrelenting pressure from those who would not be enablers became effective. The victims decided to try to end what was hurting them, fight feelings of shame enforced by the Church itself, and contradict internalized beliefs that it was unfaithfulness to tell the truth about their beloved Church. They continued fighting the institution and its resources at a personal emotional cost.

So, the Church, still in denial of its own sexual issues, moved into a "damage control" mode. It agreed to turn over "necessary" information to law enforcement authorities. Who knows how many cases it wouldn't turn over because people hadn't threatened to sue, people who were continuing to enable the sexual addiction?

That was the story as told by the mainstream press. It was cover-up and denial of a larger problem the Roman Catholic Church has with sexuality, a problem woven into the warp and woof of the institution's leadership.

The next move of denial was for official institutional representatives to target homosexuality for blame. In spite of consistent mainstream professional psychological objections to conflating homosexuality and pedophilia, projecting the problem outside the Church to an "objective disorder" that it insisted certain people have would stifle further investigation into the deeper addictive issues of the institution.

What was missing from the popular news reports, however, was significant as the Church blamed homosexuality for the problem. What was missing would put the issue in its larger context.

First, ignored in the discussion in order to blame homosexuality rather than the Church's overall attitude to sex were the complaints of priestly abuse from women. About 50% of the almost 4,000 members of SNAP (The Survivors Network of those Abused by Priests) is in fact women.

Speaking exclusively of homosexual encounters was more of what a society like ours wanted to hear. Sexism and heterosexism make the story of sexual abuse more serious when men are the victims of male sexual activity. Women are treated as less important in such matters, as if their victimhood is to be expected. Real men aren't supposed to be victims of sexual activity. They should be in charge of sexual activity.

Second, concentrating on the abuse of teenage boys plays into broader societal homophobic prejudices that connect pedophilia with homosexuality. Why are we surprised when we hear Church leaders acting as if the way to "solve" the problem is to psychologically screen out bad priests, and meaning by that those with a homosexual orientation?

Third, the fact that the sexual abuse that has come to light is associated with the Roman Catholic Church, plays into the lingering, often hidden, anti-Catholic sentiments of right-wing Protestants who are just as deeply addicted to sex. These deeply-held, long-standing anti-Catholic prejudices often surprise people, especially Catholics, who felt that past anti-Catholicism had softened.

The most right-wing of Protestants are the ones who still put down Roman Catholicism as a "cult," yet use it for their own purposes (as allies against evolution, women's reproductive freedom, women's full equality, and homosexuality) when they find it politically advantageous. Their writers produced books with titles such as *The Kingdom of the Cults* and *Chaos*

of the Cults that in their earliest editions included chapters cri-
tiquing as "cults" both Roman Catholicism and Mormonism.

The existence of widespread sexual abuse by the clergy
beyond the Catholic Church remains another societal secret.
Though, as best we can tell, it occurs in similar proportions,
it's widely swept under the rug by denominations and local
churches.

These cover-ups are successful unless media or law
enforcement get involved who are willing to break the history
of colluding with cultural Christianity and its powerful institutions. Until they do, they enable sexual and religious addiction.

A report to the Baptist General Convention in Texas in
2000 emphasized that: "The incidence of sexual abuse by clergy has reached 'horrific proportions.'" It cited studies done in
the 1980s that reported 12 percent of ministers had "engaged
in sexual intercourse with members" and nearly 40 percent
had "acknowledged sexually inappropriate behavior."

A 1993 survey by the *Journal of Pastoral Care* reported
that 14 percent of Southern Baptist ministers said they themselves had engaged in "inappropriate sexual behavior," and 70
percent said they knew a minister who had had such contact
with a parishioner. Regarding pornography and sexual addiction, one national survey disclosed that about 20 percent of
all ministers are involved in the behavior, and a 2006 survey
by the conservative Evangelical magazine *Christianity Today*
found 33 percent of pastors who responded would admit they
had visited sexually explicit websites.

In the spring of 2002, when media stories of the Roman
Catholic sexual abuse scandal were probably most numerous,
the *Christian Science Monitor* reported on the results of national surveys by Christian Ministry Resources. The story concluded that: "Despite headlines focusing on the priest pedo-
phile problem in the Roman Catholic Church, most American
churches being hit with child sexual-abuse allegations are

Protestant, and most of the alleged abusers are not clergy or staff, but church volunteers."

The number of cases of sexual abuse that actually finds its way into official reports is, of course, much smaller than the reality. Still, in 2007, three companies that insure the majority of US Protestant churches released to the Associated Press the fact that they typically receive upward of 260 reports annually of young people sexually abused by clergy, church staff, volunteers, or congregation members.

Recognizing this broader problem, SNAP in 2007 began a campaign to call attention to sexual abuse by Southern Baptist ministers. In the previous six months alone, SNAP reported receiving reports of 40 cases of sexual abuse by Southern Baptist ministers.

Even recognizing that there is a pervasive problem with sexual addiction among religious leaders who can cover their addiction with religious addiction, what's missing most from the story of clergy sexual abuse is what it says about domi- nant attitudes toward sexuality in our culture. Sex is useful economically and morally. Sex sells our products and life- styles.

Sex is a favorite conservative device to shame and demean the sexually active. Preachers have found that there's no bet- ter way to get young people to the altar of conversion than to shame them about their sexuality, their sexual activities or their sexual orientation. It just plain works.

Sexual shaming and guilt is also useful for subordinating minorities (racial, sexual, and otherwise) who are pictured as more sexually active, even dangerously so, than the "normal," "civilized," and "mature" (read white heterosexuals) among us. There's a long history of colonizers justifying the righteous- ness of their imperial designs by portraying their conquered subjects as sexually immoral while the colonizers used their subjects for their own sexual fantasies.

This is not surprising when we listen to Schaef's definition of sexual addiction — "an obsession and preoccupation with sex, in which everything is defined sexually or by its sexuality and all perceptions and relationships are sexualized." There is little question that this defines mainstream U.S. society.

SEXUAL ANOREXIA AMONG THE RELIGIOUS

Due to the influence of anti-sexual religious teachings, we've become more familiar with thinking of sexual addiction as an out-of-control search for sexual action. In that sense, pedophilia and other sexual abuse are often ways of acting out of a sexual addiction.

But what the religiously addicted may not want to face, Schaef explains, is celibacy as sexual addiction. When celibacy is a struggle that becomes obsessive, it's a sign that one is acting out of an addiction, a preoccupation and obsession with sex. And when any institution focuses on sexuality and struggles with it, that's a sign that the institution itself is promoting, even built upon, sexual addiction.

Though we've been taught to respond that celibacy is a struggle for everyone, it's actually not when it arises out of a healthy inner process that leads a person to a place where they are naturally celibate. Our larger culture might even demean such people who don't seem compulsive about sexual activity.

But denial, remember, is also a mark of an addict, and the struggle with sexuality, which our dominant institutions usually say is normal, is denial and not natural. It's the mark of an obsession that may even take the form of repulsion.

Schaef identifies a repressive sexual addiction to include persons who are obsessed with repressing sexuality, their own and other's. This includes, specifically, sexual righteousness, obsession with sexual purity, nonintegrated celibacy, and religious sexual obsession.

There is every reason to link sexual and religious addictions. Just as other addictions have often been used to justify sexual addiction, addictive religion is used more than we may want to admit to cover sexual addiction.

Conservative religion's obsession with sex and sexual repression are notorious. But, as Schaef points out: "Repression begets obsession, and obsession begets acting out." "However," she writes in *Escape from Intimacy*, "often, when our spiritual and/or political leaders act out their sexual addiction it is described as an 'indiscretion' and they are not seen as sexual addicts needing help to face recovery from a progressive, fatal, disease."

Addictions function to keep us from dealing with the issues that could change our lives. The obsession with and repression of sex and sexuality by the institutions of our culture functions as a distraction to keep society and its institutions unchanged, no matter how unhealthy the institutions are.

The collusion of religious and sexual addiction diverts attention to personal issues in a society where sex is used to sell products, comprehensive sexual education is banned, and guilt over sexuality is useful for furthering religious addiction and distracting us from the larger problems of a sexually sick culture that's economically invested in the addiction.

These cultural issues are part and parcel of sexual addiction. Carnes argues in *Out of the Shadows* that they support the dysfunctional core beliefs of sexual addicts. "The central sexual beliefs of our culture are prime ingredients," he observes, "in the addictive systems that destroy men and women and their coaddicts."

To recover from addictions requires that addicts take responsibility for the addictions and understand their addictions as addictions. Covering it with addiction to drugs or alcohol gives someone an excuse for acting out sexual addiction.

Covering sexual addiction's acting out or sexual anorexia and sexual bulimia with religious addiction justifies the obsession with control of everyone's sexuality and prevents healthy recovery. Focusing on sexual morality promotes further desperation for a righteous high to suppress the culturally common frustrations and problems people have with their own sexuality, no matter what their sexual orientation.

CHAPTER SIX

FINDING A STRONGER FIX

With the 2004 election of George W. Bush to a second term as president, leaders of right-wing religion and right-wing politics claimed to have a real Christian president of their stripe who could "save" their faith from cultural marginalization and their fears of failure. There was a jubilant high of triumph and vindication for their religious position.

Underneath, though, there continued to linger their fear that the resulting control of all branches of government by right-wing religious-political interests would be their last chance to project right-wing Christianity onto the whole country. All the polls were indicating that younger generations were less interested in the baby boomers' obsessions with gay people, guns, controlling women's sexuality, and white privilege. Impending failure loomed on the horizon, and it threatened the stash of addictive religion.

As Bill Press documents in *How the Republicans Stole Christmas*: "no sooner was President Bush reelected than red-state evangelicals claimed credit for his victory and made it clear that they expected more than mere God-talk from President Bush. They expected God-policy and God-walk as well."

Right-wing religious leaders presented their ultimatums. "Don't equivocate," Bob Jones III, president of Bob Jones University, wrote to Bush. "Put your agenda on the front burner and let it boil. You owe the liberals nothing. They despise you because they despise your Christ. Honor your Lord, and He will honor you...."

Right-wing religious/political guru James Dobson, head

of the politically powerful Focus on the Family organization based in Colorado Springs, demanded more aggressive promotion of the right-wing religious agenda or the Bush administration, he threatened, would "pay a price in four years."

What happened was the result of a unique synthesis. On the one side, political and economic conservatives — many of whom were far from being right-wing Christian in beliefs and life-styles — were reaching out to the religious right in order to push their economic agenda, as Press clearly shows. Journalist Thomas Frank in *What's the Matter with Kansas? How Conservatives Won the Heart of America* documents the use of a political strategy based on a so-called "moral values" platform that was successful in getting people to vote for a conservative economic program even against the voters' own economic interests.

"The leaders of the backlash may talk Christ," Frank argues, "but they walk corporate. Values may 'matter most' to voters, but they always take a backseat to the needs of money once the elections are won."

THREATS TO THE OLD HIGH OF RIGHTEOUSNESS

From the side of addictive right-wing religion, though, **the synthesis of right-wing religion and politics that these events represented fulfilled the progressive needs of the religious addiction**. To continue to function as an addiction, to continue to alter the underlying pessimistic mood of the addicted, the Christian right-wing needed to increase the certainty and intensity of its righteousness high. Threatened, it taught, by American culture on all sides, the feeling of righteousness could be restored and intensified by political victories, as if these victories proved they were okay.

Addictions, remember, are progressive and usually fatal to the addict. The search for a high to relieve someone of their negative self-concept is propelled toward new fixes by the feeling that the old practices aren't doing it any longer. More of the drink, more of the drug, or progression to some even stronger drug, becomes necessary to feel better about oneself.

Right-wing Christians were ripe for the picking by economic conservatives who may or may not have agreed with right-wing Christian doctrines but embraced this new political strategy that could further the high of righteousness upon which right-wing believers were dependent.

In the last forty years it had slowly became clear that the old methods of religious addiction were not working to provide a sufficient righteousness high. Right-wing Christians appeared to be losing influence, and pictured themselves as victims of those whom they felt were dominating American culture. A language of victimization dominated the emerging right-wing Christian interest in politics.

To many within the religious right, it appeared as if American and world culture were eclipsing the hope they had clung to — their religious stance. Whether it was called secularism, liberalism, inclusivism, tolerance, feminism, the gay agenda, new age religions, or multiculturalism, right-wing leaders portrayed these as real dangers they feared would be more powerful than the religion they offered.

"Culture" was seen as a threat to their faith. They spoke more and more as if they were victims of everything that was happening in the country.

There were many people who openly modeled alternative beliefs and lifestyles to that of right-wing religion and seemed to be happy without conservative Christianity. These people didn't appear to miss or need right-wing religion at all. They actually appeared successful, content, and even favored by the larger society while right-wing Christians were often portrayed as uneducated, unscientific, irrational, and backward.

Whereas being a minority within the larger culture had previously seemed to be the lot of Christians who believed Jesus' words, "narrow is the way and few there be that find it," their fears won out. The fact that they indeed might be a marginalized minority with shrinking influence threatened their normal methods for seeking the high of being the righteous.

Maybe the world out there could become the victor in the cosmic battle. What would that mean about the lordship of the god they relied on for mood alteration? Their using activities for attaining the fix weren't working any more.

The language of right-wing religious leaders was soon overflowing with fears of the threats they saw all around. The power of this language was rooted in the fear it raised in believers that the dangers were impending and extremely personal. They threatened their righteous feelings, themselves, and their very families.

Televangelist and failed Republican presidential candidate Pat Robertson's now infamous fund-raising letter to counter the Iowa Equal Rights Amendment in 1992 was a prime summary of the many sermons, televangelist specials, and fund-raising letters that played on this fear that there are threats all around to right-wing values. The embattled feeling was that right-wing Christianity was losing the "culture wars."

Amending the state's constitution to ensure equality for women was therefore an occasion for Robertson to exploit the emotions of danger that right-wing Christians were expected to feel so that seeking a political fix could now save them. "The work of a secret feminist agenda is not about equal rights for women" he wrote, touching upon as many symbols of evil as he could. "It is about a socialist, anti-family political movement that encourages women to leave their husbands, kill their children, practice witchcraft, destroy capitalism and become lesbians."

If right-wing Christianity had been considered true and God was on its side, now something was happening to threaten the sense that right-wing Christians were right and were actually going to win in the end. Televangelists and right-wing politicians could easily portray a growing fear of failure, envisioning threats to the rightness of what their followers had been counting on to save them from their rotten selves, and prescribing the need to counter all this with the battles of an all out war.

The fear was portrayed as the equivalent of a war they could lose. The opposition was not just fellow Americans who disagreed with their views but real evil "enemies" of everything the right-wing stood for. It was if they were staring Satan in the face.

By 1992, right-wing political commentator Pat Buchanan could sternly scare the religious right with the language of danger, peril, casualties, and imminent catastrophe. The foreboding picture of a religious war he painted for his audience was as frightening as the pictures of total nuclear annihilation they had feared from the 1950s up until the fall of the Soviet Union.

"There is a religious war going on in our country for the soul of America," Buchanan warned the nation on the opening night of the 1992 Republican National Convention. "It is a cultural war, as critical to the kind of nation we will one day be as was the Cold War itself."

Early Christians knew they were a minority in the Roman Empire, often a persecuted one. The Gospels picture a Jesus who had no interest in converting the Imperial government and its laws to his faith. Following Jesus included no call to become the biggest religion on earth. First and second century Christians reveled in their freedom from Caesar. Being a minority was no threat to their faith.

In fact, through much of American religious history, Christian conservatives expressed fear that government promotion of religion was dangerous for one's faith. Baptists, including Southern Baptists, led the charge for separation of Church and state.

John Leland, a well-known eighteenth-century Baptist minister, expressed this fear of an alliance of Christianity and government as follows: "Experience...has informed us, that the fondness of magistrates to foster Christianity, has done it more harm than all the persecutions ever did. Persecution, like a lion, tears the saints to death, but leaves Christianity pure; state establishment of religion, like a bear, hugs the saints, but corrupts Christianity."

Gospel meetings had previously sung hymns such as: "This world is not my home; I'm just a passin' through. If heaven's not my home, Oh, Lord what will I do." Then the world was a place of temptation, too sinful for the Church to become involved in politics.

Preachers could regularly be heard quoting the Apostle Paul's second letter to the church in Corinth (II Corinthians 6:17), "Come out from among them and be ye separate," or admonitions such as: "Be in the world but not of the world." One is reminded of the legendary Bible College that proudly promoted its isolated, rural location to parents of potential students by advertising that it was "fifty miles from any known form of sin."

Even Jerry Falwell, one of the major pushers of political crusades by right-wing Christians in recent years until his death in 2007, criticized Rev. Martin Luther King, Jr. in 1965 for King's activism, which was unattached to either political party. "Preachers are not called to be politicians, but soul winners," Falwell told his congregation back then. "Nowhere are we commissioned to reform externals." In a sermon in his church in 1965 criticizing Rev. Martin Luther King's activism he first called the civil rights movement, "the Civil Wrongs Movement."

The late twentieth-century movement of the religious right-wing into politics, which most had previously rejected as too involved in "the world," could be a more potent drug, a stronger drink. The religious right-wing quickly became dependent upon it.

The Saving High of Political Crusades and Victories

The rise of the Moral Majority and the Christian Coalition that coupled right-wing religion with conservative economic aspirations replaced the other-worldly interest of the right-wing. In the 1950s religious conservatives, social conservatives, and financial conservatives didn't get along. Conservative leaders, centering on conservative commentator William F. Buckley, Jr. consciously took on the rifts.

Working together, they were able to nominate arch-political conservative Barry Goldwater as the Republican candidate for president in 1964. His devastating lost, inspired radical economically conservative political operatives to court the religious right-wing to build a long-term movement.

As Berkeley linguist George Lakoff argues in *Moral Politics: How Liberals and Conservatives Think*, the combination of right-wing religious beliefs about the innate evil nature of human beings and the image of God as a punishing father, and the economic conservatives' belief that the proof that a person is good, moral, and disciplined is his or her economic prosperity, became a dominant frame of reference for right-wing thinking. The religious right-wing signed on to promote an Adam Smith-style Capitalist political agenda with its morality of self-interest.

The potential hope, and ultimate reality, of political wins for righteousness became the new blessed relief from facing the painful notion that they really are, as their hymns continued to remind them, "wretches," "worms," "without [even] one plea," and "deeply stained within." It vindicated their faith, themselves, and their hope of ultimate victory against the evil threat from without.

One conservative Christian and Republican political insider, David Kuo in his autobiographical *Tempting Faith* tells of the struggle of himself and others with what he calls the seduction of the political process and its victories. Kuo recounts the political processes' ability to dominate, blind those who are addicted to what is happening to others, put the seduced out of touch with their values, and allow them to be taken in by economic conservatives who were ready to use religious conservatives for an economic agenda Kuo eventually found very non-Christian.

Kuo quotes conservative Christian writer C.S. Lewis'

Screwtape Letters, as an example of knowledge he had but ignored while under the influence. In Lewis' book of fictional correspondence between a senior demon and his young protégé, "Screwtape" advises the younger tempter what to do to win the Christian victim to Satan as if he were describing this next step religious addicts took in search of a stronger high.

"Your best plan... would be to attempt a sudden, confused, emotional crisis from which he [the Christian] might emerge as an uneasy convert to patriotism....Let him begin by treating the Patriotism...as a part of his religion. Then let him, under the influence of partisan spirit, come to regard it as the most important part. Then quietly and gradually nurse him on to the stage at which the religion becomes merely a part of the 'Cause' in which Christianity is valued chiefly because of the excellent arguments it can produce in favor..."

No matter what the larger agenda was for economic conservatives though, **addictive right-wing religion came to need political battles and victories to feel righteous**. Tied directly to nationalism and the cry of "patriotism," the using activities of addictive religion now included the activities of protesting, political organizing, campaigning, fund-raising, strategizing, and dreaming of victories. These were the strategies of the new cultural war to reestablish the feeling of righteousness.

Each political victory provided the climactic high, while the fact that no addictive high lasts demanded further "values" campaigns. In the spirit of process addictions where "the action is the distraction," religio-political activity was the mood-altering process that made one feel they were not so shamefully evil after all. And the prospect of further victories offered hope that their addiction would be vindicated.

The acceptance of the belief that George W. Bush was "a good Christian man" added the new president to the list of the addiction's pushers. No matter what Bush might do in reality, the addicted couldn't come to terms with any of his administration's policy and delivery failures any more than they could face the failures of the religious leaders they had bet their high on.

Reliance on the need for Bush to be "a good Christian man in the White House," became too much a part of their addiction. No matter how he might fail to deliver what they had hoped, the need for him to be "a good Christian man" was the frame by which they didn't have to face any actions that might threaten their religio-political high.

Even when some of their own well-known writers called for a retreat from political highs, the addicted were too hooked to political fights to give up their drug. Veteran writers revered by the right-wing, Cal Thomas and Ed Dobson, in their 1999 book, *Blinded by Might* concluded that politics was too corrupt to be used to spread Christian morality in America. Along with some other Evangelicals, they recommended that conservative Christians withdraw from politics to refocus on non-political evangelism.

There was no likelihood such a cold turkey retreat could ever happen. Right-wing politics had produced too great a high to walk away from.

The opposite took place. Between 1999 and 2004, the Pew Research Center reported, the share of white Evangelicals identifying themselves with the Republican Party and its politics grew from 39 percent to 49 percent.

In the "Afterword" of his 2006 book, *Tempting Faith*, fellow conservative Kuo repeats the call for the Christian right-wing to get on the wagon by calling fellow-conservatives to "fasting from politics for a season." "I'm suggesting," he recommends, "that voting be all we do. Let's start a two-year fast. Let's take every ounce of energy we currently expend on politics and divert it to other things."

How many of his own camp will even read Kuo's book is interesting speculation. How many can abstain from this new level of addiction is another.

It's more likely that Kuo will be demonized as a traitor by the pushers of religious addiction. He'll be used as an excuse to indulge more in the activities they've now become used to for replicating their current high.

THE HOPE OF SALVATION THROUGH FAITH-BASED INITIATIVES

For example, a privatizing business model might be behind the Bush administration's funding of "faith-based initiatives." That model is justified by the claim that religious organizations can do anything more efficiently than governments. They cite no studies to prove this, however, because there are none.

We know, of course, that religious institutions pay their employees poorly in comparison to governments. They even rely on unpaid volunteer labor.

We know religious institutions can discriminate in employment of, and services to, people they believe are too sinful. We know top religious executives aren't volunteers but often well-paid bureaucrats with housing allowances and other perks such as not having to pay payroll taxes.

We know religious organizations are full of similar scandals and cover-ups as those that afflict big business. We know they have a privileged status that doesn't have to pay the property, real estate, sales, payroll, and other taxes other businesses do. We know they aren't required to publicly report what's really going on with their accounting.

But we don't hear of actual data that shows these institutions are more efficient than governments. And since full reporting isn't necessary, how could we ever really know?

We're just supposed to believe what religious leaders and their political supporters preach. That's where the faith is in government funding of "faith-based initiatives."

Instead of being expressions of faith by the churches and their supporters, "faith-based initiatives" are expressions of a growing faithlessness in the God they claimed to trust. They represent the fear that the high of righteousness needs government help.

Whereas before it was accepted that faith is to be active in good works. (C.S. Lewis once complained that Christians talk about doing "good works" but seldom about doing good work.) That meant that faithful people were to give or tithe so that there is some sort of sacrifice of their wealth. This sacrifice was the proof that God was more important to them than their money.

"Faith-based initiatives" however, allow religious people to spend tax money, other people's money — atheists', agnostics', and every taxpayer's money. That means right-wing churches can save more of their own money to build bigger estates and to feather their own nests. Their good works, then, became really other people's good works. Others now fund what were works of faith, and government becomes the factor that guarantees that right-wing religion will be successful.

Conservative Christians used to believe that there was some good, righteous, powerful, Higher Power who would see to it that the truth would win out. This God wasn't dependent upon kings or emperors for success.

"Faith-based initiatives" make government the guarantor of the success of their religion. They no longer need to trust exclusively in God or the Spirit to make things work — government will. Their Higher Power is the White House's Office of Faith-Based and Community Initiatives.

Conservative Christians used to believe that it was their job to send out missionaries and even to be missionaries themselves. If they were full-time religious professionals, they'd even have to raise their own funds from other faithful to do so.

Not any more. Taxpayer funded "faith-based initiatives" bring in the non-believers who have the economic and social needs that draw people to each initiative. The hardest part of evangelism is now the work of government funding. Religious people don't have to work as hard to "bring them in" to hear their message of salvation, or pay as much for it.

What government funded "faith-based initiatives" make clear is that those who push them have dwindling faith in their God, in themselves, or in the power of their own good works. They also demonstrate that they don't want to make the financial sacrifice that good works were supposed to take. They can keep more of their money for themselves. In other words, they've given up the real proofs that they have faith at all.

It was as early as a 1952 Supreme Court opinion when Justice Felix Frankfurter noted this lack of faith. The Court back then was being pressured to permit public schools to offer released time for students during the mandatory school attendance day so that school children could be instructed in religion by members of the clergy. Instead of the schools being closed so students could choose either to go home or attend such religious instruction, the students were expected to choose between either religious instruction classes or study hall and its equivalents in their schools.

"The unwillingness of the promoters of this [released-time religious instruction] movement to dispense with such use of the public schools," Justice Frankfurter wrote, "betrays a surprising want of confidence in the inherent power of the various faiths to draw children to outside sectarian classes — an attitude that hardly reflects the faith of the greatest religious spirits."

With government promotion of right-wing religious positions, it's the government that guarantees the righteousness of those who need the high of righteousness. Winning the battles for "faith-based initiatives" provides the new proof that the religiously addicted are okay and righteous, and that God really does like them.

Though others may argue that this use of government is bad theology, when it's become the source of the new high, addictive thinking takes over. The relief of the high is the goal, not questions of rationality about theology.

NEVER TAKING A HOLIDAY FROM PURSUIT OF THE NEXT FIX

As the religious right pushed its anti-gay, anti women's reproductive rights, anti-science, pro-profit agenda nationally and in state capitals across the nation and won, the highs were sweet fixes for the addicted. Political victories give them a comforting feeling that they're really right, okay, worthwhile, and acceptable.

Like all fixes, though, they don't last. So the addict is driven to seek another and another — another issue, another evil, another paranoiac threat to defeat. It can't ever end. Like the need for heavier doses, the causes must become bigger and more evil in the addict's mind to provide the fix. Initiatives in state legislatures such as Missouri's in 2006 to make "Christianity" (as they need their "Christianity" to be) a state's religion indicate how far the addiction has progressed.

This mind-altering fix of righteousness covers paranoid shame-based feelings about the internal and external dangers stalking them. The victim-role language of their dealers, feeds it. Like alcoholism and drug addiction, the fix numbs the religious addict against any feelings about how their addition affects others. It's a mood-altering drug.

Logically, one would think that believing they're so evil would cause the addicted to be less judgmental, more sympathetic with others. After all, one can actually find that notion in the Bible. So, in the midst of their righteous wins, they do sometimes talk sympathetically, saying to LGBT people for example: "We're all sinners."

But remember, addictions are not logical, and looking for the logic in them is a waste of time. What drives this need for winning is the high. They can't face what they believe about their rotten selves too long or they just couldn't handle it — the suppressed feelings would be bad enough to probably require anti-depressants and hospitalization.

The fix of these political wins has become an obsession. They're meant to convince the addicted that they're right and okay. Since the "high" can never last, they fall back into their feelings of fear and loathing. So they desperately need more approval, more wins. They've gotten themselves dependent upon these wins.

The need for a further cause to fight for and win is the search for relief by projecting their evil onto others.

Addictions, remember, remove the sense of responsibility. It's never the addict's fault. Addicts must be convinced they're right. Feminists, "activist judges," LGBT people, liberals, atheists, wiccans, whomever, must be understood as the real causes of the addict's problems.

The religio-political activities must continue and remain in the forefront. To maintain the high, the crusades can no longer quit.

One of the most recent yearly activities to replicate that high has become an annual holiday tradition. The process actually might remind one of comedian Stan Freberg's 1958 spoof of Charles Dickens' *A Christmas Carol* called "Green Chritma."

Freberg's Scrooge owned an ad agency geared to profiting off of Christmas. Among other ideas, the agency promoted a version of the standard ditty "We Wish You a Merry Christmas" where the last line of the well-known chorus now goes: "And please buy our beer."

FOX News began to hype this tradition annually to stir up ratings among viewers they fear might leave them in boredom to watch other networks' Christmas specials. Politically, it diverted attention to the right-wing's default — "the culture wars," and away from a failing war, a flailing president, and the next episode of the Republican culture of corruption that dominated the news. For addictive religion, FOX thereby provided justification for the addiction. It became another pusher.

One can't know how much the players on FOX are really concerned about religious issues. The actions, language, lifestyles, and writings of FOX personalities would certainly not have endeared them to right-wing religion before it sought the new high in politics. In 2005 the "war" was also hours of hype promoting sales for FOX personality John Gibson's book *The War on Christmas,* which had the typically scare-the-right-wing subtitle, *How the Liberal Plot to Ban the Sacred Christian Holiday Is Worse Than You Thought.*

The right-wing politico-religious organizations and leaders who invented the "cultural wars" in the spirit of "Onward Christian Soldiers" here had still another "war" on their hands.

The Catholic League for Religious and Civil Rights, the American Family Association, and preacher and TV personality Jerry Falwell and his Liberty Counsel, among others, launched boycotts of such retail giants as Target, Wal-Mart, and Sears. In a move that seemed fully out of touch with the spirit of "What Would Jesus Do?" they crusaded to coerce people to say "Merry Christmas" instead of the inclusive "Happy Holidays."

Since inclusivity in retailers really isn't some grand "liberal plot" but a strategy of the conservative consumerism that determines the values of U.S. culture, the right-wing's weapon was the only effective one that would make American business less tolerant of non-Christians. In this, another move not inspired by "What Would Jesus Do?," they threatened the commercial success of the season, not its rampant materialism. They decided to financially boycott seasonal commerce.

In this crusade to "Save Christmas" from the usual enemies, we see the change that reflects the new location of the fix of righteousness. I remember as a child the annual complaints from Christian pulpits that produced the slogan: "Put Christ Back in Christmas." But those were complaints in an era when right-wing religion wasn't seeking a high by being in bed with the politics of economic conservatives and consumerism. The former complaint was that the country was too commercial, the focus was on Santa Claus not Jesus, and there was too much emphasis upon shopping. It was a call to stop the commercialism, to think of something other than business.

Today, though, it's the religious and spiritual left that complains that consumerism has taken over the season and that it would be better to back away from all the profit-oriented hype and its "Black Friday" to a simpler, non-commercial spirit. Focus on our relationships and peace and good will to all, not retailing has become the left's message.

But right-wing groups became scared that business didn't affirm them. Their fear was great enough to make this an annual issue, to make this fight a source of the high that proves them righteous. So, they actively promoted the packaging of accumulating money and their faith.

They seemed to say, to contradict Jesus' claim, "You really *can* serve God and mammon." They're telling American business that there are huge profits in supporting Jesus. The price of following Jesus isn't a loss or sacrifice at all; it's a gain in the financial assets column. That's the bottom line.

It's not surprising that the dominant form of Christianity that developed in the US had to adjust to bless our economic system, and has spent plenty of time justifying that adjustment. Theologians have developed all sorts of interpretations to protect America's profit-oriented soul.

You're never going to get the wealthy Americans who have most to contribute in the pews if you preach that today they should live by such sayings of Jesus as: "Give all you have to the poor and follow me" or "It's harder for a rich man to enter the kingdom of heaven than a camel to go through the eye of a needle." Those messages would be economic downers.

And you're never going to get any preacher with faith in Capitalism as their Higher Power — no matter how much they quote the Old Testament to support other prejudices — to take literally the oft-repeated Old Testament command never to loan money and ask for interest. Too much of the Almighty Dollar is made through collecting interest and dividends.

In American Christianity you can post the Ten Commandments with its: "Thou shalt not take the name of the Lord thy God in vain," and then believe that it's really not a vain thing to put God's name on a nation's money. You can even take pride in the righteousness of the whole country for doing it.

FOX political talk-show host Bill O'Reilly saw visions of profits dancing in the heads of retailers if they'd just promote the homeless Jew of Nazareth who was born of an unwed, Palestinian, teenage mother. "Every company in America should be on their knees thanking Jesus for being born," he told viewers of FOX's "Your World with Neil Cavuto" on November 30, 2005. "Without Christmas, most American businesses would be far less profitable. More than enough reason for business to be screaming, 'Merry Christmas.'"

The pushers once again stirred up the culture warriors, the season was again profitable, and "Christmas" was forced on the lips of retailers in order for them to cash in on the season. The televangelists and preachers could take long winter's naps knowing that their offering plates, too, were fuller because they've fought and won the battle to sell "Christmas."

By so moving the source of the righteous high to political and now even business victories, the Christian right-wing has worked to correct Jesus' claim that Caesar and God represent two separate allegiances. They needed addictively to seek Caesar's buttressing of their faith. God needs government subsidy. It's a cultural war after all. God should be more patriotic.

All of this shows the dwindling ability of the Christian right to believe in their God. All of it shows that the old highs aren't working to assuage their fear and guilt.

They don't count on God and the Church to change the world or be victorious. They buy the "Left Behind" books and videos to bolster their faith, to assure them that all will be well. They count on government and taxpayers to promote and fund their faith, not their own good works, their own contributions, or their faith that their God is capable.

What we're seeing in their faith in the government promotion of faith-based good works, the State advancing laws and amendments to force people to act "Christian," and trust in retailers to sell Christmas, is not only the end of right-wing belief. It's the wearing out of the right-wing high of righteousness. And that is evidence that the addict might be getting closer to hitting bottom.

The danger is that their fear will overwhelm the non-addicted if the non-addicted aren't pursuing their own health but are taking care of the feelings of the addicted. Yet, it's the need of addictive right-wing religion for further fixes that's setting the national agenda.

The desperation of political and business victories is rooted in addictive right-wing religion's unbelief, which is rooted in their fear of coming down from the old highs of righteousness. It's motivating one cause after another in the "culture wars" that they've constructed. But this can only happen if there are others outside the addiction who are too afraid to intervene and instead enable addicts so they never experience the misery and insight of what they need — to hit bottom.

CHAPTER SEVEN
WHEN LIBERALS ARE ENABLERS

I watched the TV panel uneasily, cringing at times. In the past year, the right-wing minister of a suburban mega-church had grabbed the spotlight of local and national media attention by pushing a successful amendment to his state's constitution to ban marriage equality for gay citizens. Even that righteous victory and the attention he and his church received couldn't be enough for him, of course.

This right-wing Christian leader on the panel said such things as "polarization is good for the country," during an exchange with an intelligent, kind liberal minister whose very liberalism couldn't let him agree with the idea that divisiveness was valuable. Liberals, after all, are surely the ones who feel the rational and sensible thing to do is to seek common ground. They're often convinced that if people just understood each other, everybody would get along.

Though their disagreement was obvious and that right-wing religious advocate of polarization seemed to be taking an extremely unpopular position, the liberal was still losing. The high of the right-winger's past political victory for righteousness, constant mainstream media attention, and now the taking of a lone stand for God's truth on public television against a liberal minister who wrote a popular column for a mainstream daily newspaper couldn't fail to be an adrenalin-producing, mood-altering combination for a religious leader if he were also a religious addict. What a rush to stand for righteousness!

The liberal was no TV match for the driven, righteous passion of the right-winger. His kindness and understanding couldn't break through the realities of the hostile rhetoric that ignites the righteous highs the addicted have become dependent upon in their political crusades and their victories today.

That's not to say that the liberal minister didn't have his facts straight, or that his arguments weren't more cogent. He was, it seemed, arguing on solid grounds to keep US society open for the multiplicity of citizens' voices on moral values. He had even come prepared for arguments using the Bible. And he was an experienced communicator — writing his popular newspaper column on the diversity of religious understandings of religious, social, and political issues.

The communication problem was that he was arguing the way nice liberals are supposed to do. Unlike the right-wing preacher, he didn't use soundbites, interrupt, put down his opponent's arguments as mere "parroting" of some hackneyed position, dismiss the arguments as anti-faith, "radical" or "out of touch," or respond by saying that that's just how "you people" argue. The liberal minister was polite, reasoned, and inoffensive to everyone. And, as a progressive friend of mine commented, the right-winger ate him alive.

Though the right-wing minister continued to put down both of the more liberal panelists with name-calling, arrogance, and provocative remarks, no one was ready to point those tactics out, confront him, or, frankly, take the chance of offending the offender, especially in public. No one would say, "Wow, to make those statements, sounds arrogant and condescending," even though he was arrogant and condescending. The moderator wouldn't, and both the panel's liberals were just awfully, awfully nice.

I would guess that most of us would prefer nice. We'd pick nice people who work very hard not to hurt our feelings to include in our circle of friends any day.

Yet, at this stage in our culture's broad-based enabling of religious addiction, media expectations have changed along with the ruthlessness of polarized politics. The right-wing itself has seen to that.

Addictiveness, after all, does that. It's tied to the feeling of its righteous cause so desperately that little matters in comparison with replicating that high. No cost is eventually too great.

In their advanced stage of religious addiction, religious addicts seem unable to feel in any depth how those not caught up in the addiction are hurt by the right-wing's words and actions. They don't fathom, for example, how governmental prayers "in Jesus' name" are insensitive to others. The "high" that such prayers produce for them feels more important and vital than how any other people might feel as a result.

Hurting the feelings of others even seems justified — it might hook those whom they hurt so they also turn to addictive religion for relief from the very hurts the addicts pile onto them. And if they do convert, their embracing of the right-wing cause feels like a justification of the addiction to the addict. It's another righteous victory.

Nice, therefore, has to be redefined by those outside the addiction in order to intervene in these new right-wing patterns. Nice is not the same as being fair or kind, after all.

ADDICTS THRIVE ON LIBERAL ENABLING

Poet Robert Frost is credited with an observation that gets to the heart of liberal enabling of this addiction: "A liberal is a man too broadminded to take his own side in a quarrel." Liberals often leave others with the impression that they don't really stand for, or value, anything very deeply.

Not so the right-wing in religion and politics today. Right-wing people speak as the convinced. They cover up any personal doubts by arguing as if they have no doubt at all.

They don't hem and haw. They don't deal in subtleties. They're clear about who the enemies are — liberals, secularists, feminists, gays, humanists, the American Civil Liberties

Union, etc. You know the current list. And they treat them as targets.

To speak as the convinced is to speak as "us" versus "them" in generalizations about "those people." It's harder for the religiously addicted to consider that their list of targets includes actual living, breathing, vulnerable human beings in each category they condemn who don't fit their stereotypes. The impersonal nature of right-wing discussions of people and the use of caricatures keep any chance of them feeling that there are real, emotional, even deadly human consequences for what they do and say, at bay.

They get their key, consumer-tested talking points from think-tanks located in Colorado Springs, Virginia Beach, and Lynchburg. They're trained in soundbites. Remember, much of right wing religious talk really is the kind of jargon and soundbites that functions as what John Bradshaw identifies as mystification in the language of addicts. It's meant to paralyze the discussion, not further or deepen it.

Notice again how right-wing religious leaders always come back to the same, often coded, historically meaningless, and mystifying wording that the spin-doctors from their think tanks have carefully worked out for them — family values, pro-life, partial-birth abortion, marriage protection, Americanism, patriotism, God, war on Christians, war on Christmas. Important to right-wing religious politics, just as it was important to right-wing religious-speak before, is the repetition of the same mystifying words and phraseology when speaking of an issue. It's what politicians call "message discipline."

Liberals, on the other hand, try to think and speak in nuance. They weigh the alternatives, recognizing that there often are more than two sides to any issue, that things are seldom reducible to the either/or that's central to addictive thinking. They tend to be concerned with the content of language and actually exploring various ways to provide better understanding. They pay less attention to repetition. It seems shallow and doesn't further any discussion.

Yet the mainstream media has evolved to the point that it peddles mostly coping mechanisms for, not insight into, society's problems. So, in this day of seven-second media soundbites, which do you think people remember most, whether they agree or not? The considered points made by a liberal who weighs the subtleties: "Well, there's this to consider and then this, if not this." Or a simplistic right-wing soundbite such as: "It's Adam and Eve, not Adam and Steve."

What's your favorite liberal soundbite, one that you hear repeated throughout the country by most liberals? Liberals believe that educating people, answering the questions they ask, and not repeating catchphrases constitutes honest communication. When they come up with what could be a soundbite, they abandon it quickly. They believe a question deserves an answer that helps the questioner come to their own informed conclusions.

Granting such good intentions, why are there liberals who continue to enable the right-wing by letting them set the political, religious and social agenda, the terms of the debates, and the language of religion, instead of uncompromisingly confronting right-wing offenses? Why do they enable the right-wing by refusing to call untruths lies, by hoping not to make the addicted feel bad, or acting as if liberals have no uncompromising values? Why are there liberals who continue to act as if what's wrong with right-wing people is the fault of liberals because liberals haven't "understood" the right-wing well, included them more, been nice enough to them, or reached out to them enough?

THE DISABLING EFFECT OF LIBERAL GUILT

Liberals often seem to be ineffective because they're plagued by a liberal guilt. They don't want to repeat offenses from the past. They know such offences existed and don't want to deny them. They know there's been discrimination and that often their own groups have historically been the culprits in white racism, sexism, heterosexism, even classism — though classism is tough for many otherwise liberal folk.

Liberals don't want to repeat the sins of their ancestors, nor do they want to be dogmatic and absolutist the way right-wingers are. They believe all human beings are struggling together.

Yet, there's something else. It's as if they need to atone for the oppressions of the past, to make up for them by avoiding anything that would be offensive to anyone at all in the present, even if the potentially-offended religious right-wing continues its destructive addictive activities and the resulting oppression of others. Addicts of any substance or process know how to play on such guilt.

Guilt-feeling liberals believe that the right-wing should be given equal time for their arguments — they'll even provide it, as if the right-wing doesn't already dominate most of the time in most of the media. The 2007 study by the watchdog group Media Matters for America found that conservative religious leaders were not only quoted, interviewed, or mentioned 3.8 times more often than progressive religious leaders on the three major TV networks, the three major cable news channels, and PBS, but 2.7 times more often even in the nation's major newspapers.

Liberals feel that the views of the right wing should actually be respected. They don't want to say that people can be respected but not the views one rejects as false, hurtful, and offensive. They want to appear understanding about the personal circumstances that produce such bigotry in people whom they don't believe are inherently bigots.

They're afraid that they might come across as too dogmatic, or as if they believe too much in absolute values, or that they'll appear just as arrogant as the right-wing. They don't want to say that they believe an idea is wrong. And to be nice, they don't want to offend the people who are still offending them.

Guilt-feeling liberals cringe when another liberal does state the blatant, unvarnished truth. They distance themselves from any other liberal who says: "The Emperor has no clothes." They're some of the quickest critics of passionate left-wing activists.

The result of liberal guilt and its accompanying hesitancy is that liberals appear to believe in nothing sincerely. To outside observers they look as if they are passionate about nothing.

They act as if values such as equal opportunity and compassionate treatment for all human beings, ending the abuse of everyone, and trying to do no harm are negotiable. Sometimes they're okay, they seem to say. They act as if all values and ideas should be respected no matter how destructive and hurtful they are.

Right-wing critics are quick, therefore, to paint liberals as aloof, relativist, wishy-washy, flip-floppers, who are easily gullible and stand for nothing. It's, in fact, so easy for them to do. And many of the addicted right-wing believe liberals are valueless.

How to Enable an Addiction

When liberals take such a guilt-ridden stance toward the religiously addicted, they are practicing what addiction specialists call enabling, co-addiction, or codependency. Along with the denial of the addicts themselves, though, these liberal enablers are crucial for maintaining religious addiction.

It's not about judgment or mean-spiritedness. Those who function as enablers of an addiction, remember, are often the closest people to the addict. They really do care about the addict. They're not bad or stupid people. They don't picture themselves as the addicted one's enemies. They're most often family members.

Many addiction specialists are convinced that the most comprehensive way to treat an addiction is to treat it as a family system problem, as I noted briefly before. All the members of the family, they tell us, maintain an environment that supports the addiction because these family members aren't facing their own emotional needs and issues.

Family system specialists often compare the family to a mobile. The members of a family interact to keep the mobile in balance and thus they adapt to the addiction. To step out of a balance that maintains the addiction is to force others to change so as to rebalance the mobile, maybe even send the addicted member to seek recovery.

Family members enable an addiction when they refuse to recognize that a drunk family member is an alcoholic. The alcoholic member doesn't want to admit the problem. It would require a whole new approach to life. But, as Abraham Twerski advises: "Remember this, for it is important: *Identification of addictive thinking must come from outside the addict.*"

Family enablers, however, don't want to admit to themselves and each other that the family member is addicted. They'll leap to every excuse in the book to deny the addiction. Seriously naming the addiction would require a new approach to the alcoholic. Even though that approach would improve the family dynamic and stop colluding with the addiction, the enablers are in a sense addicted to, dependent upon, the addict.

They know the addict will get angry, even threatening and violent, if they point out the elephant everyone knows is dominating the living room. Wanting to be nice and to not upset things, they adjust the family's life to compensate for, work around, not offend, and cover up for the addict. They might seek other understandings of the drinking that don't require it to be faced as an addiction. The addiction is often treated as a great family secret, never spoken of, certainly not in public.

The addict is thus the center of the family's dynamics. The addict sets the agenda and most of what the family members do is in response to the addiction.

In some cases family members become stuck harping upon the problem, complaining about the problem to other members of the family, and living in anger or a hidden rage that can produce their own physical ailments. They will even sit around with others constantly rehearsing the offenses of the addict, thus finding allies for comfort, without doing what it takes to change the dysfunctional dynamic.

It's more likely that enablers routinely, day in and day out, are quite active in their own denial. Cleaning up the addict's messes, putting up with the addict's rage and offensive actions, defending the addict against critics, making excuses for the addict to other family members and to the outside world, and bailing the addict out of the consequences of the addiction become standard operating procedures that eventually seem to be just normal, "nice," family living.

Even if it starts to feel like martyrdom and self-sacrifice, somehow enabling behaviors seem to be what must be done. Religious teachings can promote it as if it's healthy. How many enablers are convinced that it's their religious duty to keep the addict from the consequences of the addiction? Biblical verses such as "Greater love has no man than he give up his life for his friends," provide useful excuses even though enabling is more about how the enabler feels about him or herself rather than what the loving thing for the addict, but upsetting thing for the enabler, would be.

While the addict embarrasses, offends, demeans, jeopardizes, and abuses family members, upsetting the family applecart is just too much for enablers. Smoothing things over feels as if it's the better thing to do.

Blaming themselves and other family members for the addict's behavior substitutes for blaming the addict. Enablers may argue among themselves about whose fault it is while the addict is more than ready to agree that it's anyone and anything but the addict's fault.

We're familiar with the language of an enabler's blame and guilt. It sounds like the reasons an abused spouse gives for staying with the abuser —

If only the addict had an easier life....

If only I were more understanding....

If only I were more loving....

If only I didn't do things to upset the addict....

If only I could change the addict...

If only the addict understood the harm she/he were doing....

If only I tried different methods...

If only I could sit down and explain things....

If only I emphasized more of the addict's good qualities....

If only I were better, nicer, smarter, perfect.

Enabling behavior depends upon the enabler not understanding that Al-Anon principle for those who must deal with an addict. It's those Three C's — You did not Cause it, you cannot Control it, and you cannot Cure it. Not embracing the Three C's prevents change from happening because it focuses attention on the addict and the addiction, not on the health of the enablers.

ADDICTIVE RELIGION SETS THE AGENDA

We can recognize all of this as the activity of enablers of addictive religion as well. As liberal religion lost its ability to set the cultural agenda to addictive religion, addictive religion began to set the agenda in the larger cultural family with liberals left to respond to that agenda.

In the early 20th century, addictive religion was being culturally marginalized, and its leaders sensed it. Many identified themselves as conservative Christians, "Fundamentalists," and "Conservative Evangelicals" who defined themselves in opposition to liberal Christianity. Liberal religion in the form of nineteenth century liberalism and the "Social Gospel" were considered more respectable alternatives that in the American class structure were often identified with the upper classes. Fundamentalists were often pictured as outside the educated, influential, and prosperous mainstream of America.

Liberal and progressive Christianity and the Social Gospel movement were prominent in the late 19th century and early

20th century in the Unites States. Together they became the dominant position in mainline churches until the last half of the 20th century. Fundamentalism developed in reaction to this movement but was being rejected as reactionary, ineffective, out-dated, anti-science, insular, and unconcerned with social ills.

Liberal Christianity stressed the importance and value of an individual's freedom of thought and expression in religion and life. The Social Gospel was a practical outcome of this liberal theology. It applied what they were convinced were Christian principles to social problems such as poverty, alcohol and drugs, racial tensions, poor living conditions, inadequate schools, and war.

One of the most important and influential books in the twentieth century reflected the thrust of the Social Gospel. In 1896, a Congregational minister from Topeka, Kansas, Charles Sheldon, wrote a widely read novel entitled *In His Steps* that sold multi-millions of copies, was translated into scores of languages, and even appeared in newspapers, magazines, and comic books. Sheldon was committed to Christian Socialism and identified with the Social Gospel. In his work he coined the motto: "What would Jesus do?"

So culturally influential were liberal Christianity and the Social Gospel that they became a basis for Franklin Delano Roosevelt's New Deal, the American Civil Rights Movement for racial justice, and Liberation Theology in Roman Catholicism, which sought justice for the poor especially in Latin America.

This was all a threat to reactionary religious conservatism, Fundamentalism, and Conservative Evangelicalism. One can hear in their claims of "success" today the sense of triumph over this previous marginalization, dismissal, and demeaning by the larger culture. This very late twentieth-century sense of "success," understood in their growing numbers and becoming "mainstream," feeds their new high. It's the assurance that they're really righteous.

The search for the stronger fix by those addicted to a religious high moved from internally responding to these liberal movements to the political sphere. With the cooperation of the political right-wing, right-wing religious leaders using language that arose from their fear that they were victims of liberal Christianity added to conservative religious practices the thrill, mental distractions, busywork, and emotions of the political sphere. These became the new mood-altering using activities.

As they became more public and political in their goals, the right-wing took the offensive, gained attention beyond their numbers, and used newfound political friends and funds to set the agenda to which liberal religion and politics would have to respond. The addicted became the center of the family system that is the broader cultural system. Being "born again" was now respectable even though it was a more moderate president, Jimmy Carter, who openly and unabashedly used the term politically.

Until the political victories of the right-wing began, it was easy for the more liberal mainstream religious thought to dismiss fundamentalism, conservative evangelicalism, and other right-wing religious movements as reactionary, lower-class, unscientific, behind the times, anti-education, deluded, and ignorant. It was easy to joke about those folks or ignore or pity them. Many who populated the atheist, agnostic, more liberal Christian, and other religious and anti-religious movements had personally fled from such conservative religious backgrounds.

Enabling reactions were often a part of the response. After ignoring the condition in the hope that it would go away, liberals began to wake up in alarm. They spoke with each other about the activities and actions of religious addicts. They rehearsed again and again the actions of the religious addicts but did little about them.

The religious addicts set the national political agenda. Liberal activists found themselves on the defensive in a world where they were previously making progress. They became busy responding to one initiative after another at local, state, and federal levels to restrict women's reproductive choice, the equal rights of LGBT people, affirmative action, public education, non-faith-based safety nets for the poor and disabled, the separation of church and state, and equal rights for non-Conservative Christians and people of other faiths.

The pushers of religious addiction with the help of other right-wing politicos learned to control the language of the discussion. Their followers picked up this new religious-political language as easily as they had adopted for three-quarters of a century the mystifying, thought-stopping religious jargon of their churches

Liberal respondents were on the defensive and argued using this same language. George Lakoff has studied and written extensively about the development and power of the repetition of the language and framing of the religious right and the danger of each repetition of this language even to deny it. Everybody thought about former President Richard Nixon as a "crook," even his friends, the moment he addressed the nation on TV in response to the Watergate events and said, "I am not a crook."

It was easy for addictive religion to push back against liberal responses. They took the initiative in defining what Christianity is, leaving out all those who claimed to be Christians but didn't agree with their conservative theology and political agenda. They portrayed the liberal, often called "mainstream," churches as dying because their message was out-of-touch and plain wrong.

Liberals were too caught up in "nice" and "polite" to respond in kind, to say that what right-wing Christianity is saying is wrong, that it's understanding of the Bible or the Church is wrong and harmful. So, the right-wing could respond, "See, they don't stand for anything. They're situation ethicists."

BULLYING AND BLAMING LIBERAL RELIGION

The next step was for the addicts to blame the enablers. They knew how hard it was for liberals to blame them, or anyone. All evil in the world today, addictive religion said, has been caused by liberalism, including liberal religion, either directly or by liberals allowing people to get away with evils.

Right-wing religion was in fact a victim, they said, of liberals and their "religions." Speaking as victims, any criticism was portrayed as persecution, as Thomas Frank documents. "The disproportion between dish-it-out and take-it is positively staggering," he writes. But the religious and political right-wing knew that the accusation was enough to bully most liberals, especially the liberally religious.

When liberals did respond, right-wing religion knew how easy it was to further bully liberal religion into submissiveness. When pro-equality forces decided to stand up and say that "Hate is Not a Family Value," the right-wing stood up straight, acted offended, and bullied them by saying, "You're not accusing us of hate speech, are you?"

Liberals didn't want to offend and say, "Yes, we are. The words you use from the pulpit are the same words bigots use when they torture and kill gay people." Instead, many liberals quit using the phrase as if hate suddenly in their minds could possibly be a family value.

It was easy politically, then, to portray the religious and political left as having no values. And to the extent that liberals continued to believe that right-wing religion flowed from lack of intelligence, good breeding, or country bumpkinness, it was easy to portray liberals as elite, latté-drinking, east coast snobs.

LIBERAL RELIGION PEERS OUT OF ITS CLOSET

The signs of change, however, are only beginning to appear. A "Network of Spiritual Progressives" formed around the work of author and rabbi Michael Lerner. Its May 2006 four-day conference attracted participants from 39 states.

Reporting on a recent national yearlong survey in *A New Spiritual Home: Progressive Christianity at the Grass Roots*, religion professor Hal Taussig describes and assesses the rise of progressive religious activity below the surface of mainstream press reports of fading mainline denominations and right-wing religious-political dominance.

These churches and para-churches are characterized, Taussig notes, by:

- vitality and expressiveness in their spiritual practices

- insistence on intellectual integrity

- transgression of gender and sexual orientation boundaries

- belief that Christianity can be vital without claiming to be the best or only true religion

- strong commitments to social justice and environmentalism

This collection of progressive grassroots congregations and organizations that have rejected right-wing religion is just discovering itself. As these groups learn that they aren't alone, they could begin to stand up for their values and very lives against the religious addiction.

The Unitarian Universalist Church has experimented successfully with advertising. This "Uncommon Denomination," whose historically liberal faith has saved many a desperate ex-fundamentalist soul, began asserting the presence of its alternative approach to faith, values, and humanity through billboard and media advertising.

The United Church of Christ has gotten more publicity than ever with its commercials proclaiming that it turns no one away. When NBC and CBS were too afraid of the addicted and refused to air the UCC's boldest commercials, they proved that these ads were exactly what a sick, enabling culture needed.

It took decades for liberal religion to think of itself highly enough to open its closet door and begin to challenge the monopoly on Christianity trumpeted by right-wing churches. Maybe the triumph of right-wingers in the presidential and congressional races from the 1990s through 2004 finally made it sink in. Liberal religion realized that it had better speak up or forever be shut out of the national debate and American life.

Liberal religion says none of this has to be — there is another way. It sees the problem as systemic, rooted in the teachings of the cultural institutions that we worship. It doesn't see it rooted in the Divine, the Universe, or something unhealable in human nature.

Liberal religion sees that things can change and that people are fully capable of changing things. We don't have to wait for some inhuman cataclysm. We don't have to believe that war, poverty, and crime are inevitable and will always be with us.

Its leaders tap into the history of critique of conservative religion and politics that's found as far back as the Hebrew prophets and the Jesus of the Gospels. Just as Martin Luther King Jr, did, they see this tradition as a call against the actions and abuse of the religiously addicted and the political leaders in bed with them.

These prophets took on not the sex lives of every-day people, but the lifestyles of the rich, governments, and conservative religious leaders of their day who were often reinforcing each other's moves to disenfranchise the poor and others who didn't bow to the leadership of the priesthood.

The words of the eighth-century prophet Amos are a clear example of intervention in the conservative religion of his day. They were favorites of Dr. King, and they're not "nice."

"I hate, I despise your religious feasts; I cannot stand your assemblies," was God's word to the conservative religious and political leaders, Amos said. "Even though you bring me burnt offerings and grain offerings, I will not accept them. Though you bring choice fellowship offerings, I will have no regard for them. Away with the noise of your songs! I will not listen to the music of your harps. But let justice roll on like a river, righteousness like a never-failing stream."

In today's culture, liberal religion is a radically different way of looking at things than that found among the right-wing and its cultural supporters. It's outside the dominant voice that right-wing religion has gained. That means it must, as Dr. King, knew, stand up against right-wing forces, the conservatives in his day who fought to maintain segregation and discrimination.

Standing in opposition to addictive religion, he taught, also means that the mainstream will consider someone who does so a threat to the addictions that society now supports. King therefore expected that those who fight these coping mechanisms of society and its institutions would be accused of being unable to adjust to reality.

No wonder, then, that he said in his 1963 *Strength to Love*: "The saving of our world from pending doom will come not through the complacent adjustment of the conforming majority, but through the creative maladjustment of a nonconforming minority."

Until recently liberal religion hasn't acted as if it really believed. It's been hesitant to stand firmly, publicly, and boldly on the alternative vision it offers. It's been too hesitant to speak up and proudly claim that it believes right-wing theology is plain wrong. It's been enabling.

Maybe liberal religion hasn't felt worthy enough to stand up to the addict — until now. Addicts often require what's been called intervention. The ones who care most about the addict often must have the courage to confront the addict and say they are opposed to the addiction. But when they decide to do so they must do this not to control or cure the addict but to protect and promote the health of all those outside, but affected by, the addiction.

Chapter Eight

Toward an Intervention

Abraham Twerski observes, "Since addiction involves a distortion of perception, only some major event or series of events can make the addict question the validity of his or her perception." The events that produce this change help the addict "hit bottom."

Rock bottom experiences result in a change of perception in which the addict effectively concludes that life is worse with the addiction than without it. This change of perception requires, of course, that the addict continues to believe that it's possible that his or her own life really *can* be better without the addiction.

Changing their perception in this way is more difficult for religious addiction than most other addictions. That's because, central to the beliefs of addictive religion, which those who embrace it have internalized, is its ideologies of the nature of evil and of the evil nature of human beings.

To join the religion, a follower must have first been emotionally convinced by the religion that there is no human hope for healing on earth for both the problems of world evil as well as their own personal depravity. That means they're convinced that life can't be any better without the addiction.

Coping All the Way to Rock Bottom

Addictive religion is religion as a way merely to cope with human problems, not heal them. Only a Heavenly Father can change the world, it teaches, and He will only do that at the end of time. When this idea is taken seriously, it has convinced believers that all they can do is cope, put up with things, and wait for the afterlife or the end of times. It's disempowering while it's supposed to still make them feel better.

War will always be with you. People will always cheat you. Others will tempt your faith. The devil will constantly try to intervene. None of this will really improve no matter how those misguided, non-believing do-gooders try to change things. So, you must do everything you can do to cope with the inevitable.

You yourself will always be evil, it says. You will always be prone to do terrible things that deserve punishment. That's how you are now constructed. You can't expect anything better from yourself on your own without the addiction.

You should never expect to have a better self-concept. Don't even try. That would be pride or some heresy like "New Age Religion."

Your only hope now, in spite of the innateness of your deepest problems, is to be saved from the eternal punishment of hell personally and from the global "Tribulation" that God will bring on the whole earth at the end times for those who do believe society can be healed. The best you can do is cope with your badness and the lost world that's just this way. Only God will solve your ultimate problems and it won't happen in this life.

This is religion using what Schaef calls "the process of the promise," which is a part of all addiction. Addictions look to the future without recognizing and dealing with the present. It will get better somewhere in the future, whether that's the tomorrow that's always tomorrow or, for addictive religion, the end of time or eternal life after death.

The present is the place for the fix that provides the high, not for healing. The promise that all will be right and we'll get all we need is always to be fulfilled in the future. "There is no group in our society more adept at this process," Schaef points out, "than the church, for one of the major premises is that of eternal life."

With such an emotional and lifestyle commitment to the

belief that evil can't be cured in place in many religious people, it's surprising how many people still do free themselves
from addictive religion. This is a clear sign that they weren't
yet caught up in the religion as an addiction. They were more
like social drinkers. They still could listen to, and think sober-
ly about, a good, open discussion of the facts of the matter.

Others might leave addictive religion and be what recovery groups call "dry drunks." They abandon the leaders, institutions, and communities that push the addiction, but spend
the rest of their lives obsessed with the addiction, angry with
the addicted, and never examining the underlying reasons
why they had used religion as an addiction. To continue to
cope, they might substitute another addiction.

Still others leave addictive religion and do their own internal psychological work to confront the negative self-images
and hurts from the past that made addictive religion appealing to them in the first place. These might participate in the
equivalent of Fundamentalists Anonymous, non-addictive
religious communities, or other forms of positive healing. The
more they do so, they also become less likely to be enablers
of the addiction.

The natural course of addictions is that they are progressive and lead to hitting rock bottom unless someone interferes
to sooth or remove some of the distress that the addiction produces. That's what those outside the addiction do, often with
good intentions, enabling the addict to remain more comfort-
ably addicted. Often even their attempts to fight, control, or
cure the addict are acts of enablement for they actually keep
addicts from being in touch with their emotions.

Hitting bottom isn't pretty or a joy to watch. To the extent
that others are caught up in the addict's life, dependent upon
the addict, they'll fear that they too will be deeply hurt by
the addict's rock bottom experience. They too must evaluate
whether the addiction or the pain of the process of ending the
addiction is more beneficial to them and future generations.

The end of religious addiction in the dominant form it is

today will not come, quickly, easily and without pain, but it can come at almost anytime now. A direct intervention that forces religious addicts off to treatment for the causes of their addiction is currently, however, counter-cultural.

Our cultural institutions thrive on addictions. They both participate in and reward enabling. The partnership of corporate-sponsored political conservatism and its accompanying corporate media with the religiously addicted puts most of the economic incentive behind maintaining this and other addictions. Coping mechanisms currently sell.

So, confronting religious addiction means no longer cooperating with it in any way. And when enablers stop cooperating, the addicts and those who continue as enablers will blame these actions of non-cooperation, not the addiction, for creating a crisis, a crisis that will threaten "rock bottom" for the addict.

When Martin Luther King Jr. talked about non-violent non-cooperation and its direct action, he knew that the very actions that stopped the enabling of the system would provoke a crisis for the system. "Nonviolent direct action," King wrote in "Letter from a Birmingham Jail," "seeks to create such a crisis and foster such a tension that a community which has constantly refused to negotiate is forced to confront the issue. It seeks so to dramatize the issue that it can no longer be ignored...."

For King, stopping the enablement of the disease was the most loving thing to do. He also knew it would provoke a crisis with which the community would have to deal.

ENABLERS NO MORE

So, what can we do to protect our society and ourselves, maintain our sanity, promote a healthy alternative, and confront religious addiction when we cannot control or cure the addict? What's the closest thing to what recovery groups call an intervention when we're dealing with the advanced, destructive form of religious addiction that's become culturally dominant?

(1) Dealing with the addiction must focus on saving oneself first, not the addict.

It often involves the sadness of watching the addict crash and burn. But the reason to deal with the addiction cannot be to change the addict. It must always be to take care of one's own life, community, and health.

The reason to confront an addiction is self-centered. It's finally giving up any desire to control, change, or cure the addict.

It takes massive inner strength and a good self-concept. It cannot arise out of the same negative evaluation of ourselves that the religious right-wing shares. It requires a personal confrontation with all of our own feelings of guilt, and an evaluation of where in our past they were installed in us.

• **It means that we must clean up our own relationships to religion.**

This might be the hardest task to undertake, and we might not want to do so. We might even prefer to deny we need to do so. But, our goal is our own health and therefore we must ask and honestly answer the question: Are we healthy about our relationship to religion?

Growing up in America means we've been exposed to religious abuse. A person doesn't have to be brought up religiously to experience its results.

Door-to-door and media-dominating religious salespeople who are expected to fulfill their quota of testifying, confront others with their own coping mechanisms. Everybody, it's been said, loves a lover. It's not unusual for anyone to share personal stories of the people and things they love. But a compulsion to make people become like them, or a need to "witness" out of fear of punishment or a Father's disfavor is a different thing. Such testifying is annoying and a user activity by which addicts seek their next fix, proof that they're really righteous after all. Again, as AA says: "The action is the distraction."

The airwaves are full of the condemning and fiery, judg-mental words of televangelists, radio preachers and right-wing experts. Radio station after radio station, television stations, and cable channels, and even newspaper religious columns are dedicated to the spreading of the negative theology that traces itself through Augustine and the lifestyle issues embed-ded in his theology. It's the rare individual who can walk away from these forces without anger, bitterness, or guilt, though many at times are able to hide these feelings well.

• **Whether religious or not, we must ask ourselves frankly whether we are we still fighting our pasts.**

Do we respond to the addicts with a relaxed attitude of learning and free choice? Or do we respond with resentment, fear, the need to win, and anger?

If a healthy approach to life is to face every event in a relaxed manner as a learning experience, do we know why we don't approach religious addicts that way? Though there are many reasons to get angry with the destructive attitudes and actions of the pushers of religious addiction who domi-nate the scene today, how does such anger prevent us from responding in more creative ways?

If a religious person tells me I'm going to hell, how do I respond? Do I become angry, resentful and defensive as if their beliefs really are more than just their problem? Or do I think, and even say, something like: "That's an interesting idea? Tell me how hell functions in your life for you?"

If a religious person tells me that all humans are evil, lost, depraved, and deserving of hell, do I become angry and defensive and thereby get caught up in their addiction? Or do I ask something like: "That's interesting. Tell me how evil you are?"

When they respond to these questions in an addictive manner, do I state my own beliefs without argument and then allow myself to walk away? "Sorry, you and I really do dis-agree about all this."

Or do I get caught up in a contest with them to prove to

them (or ourselves) that I'm right? Once I have moved to the feeling that I must "win" the argument, I've moved out of a response that's healthy for me. I've moved into a place where I need to stop to ask why the event has turned into a competitive contest with an addict. And why does winning a contest with this addict make a difference to me?

A relaxed attitude of learning allows someone to become creative in their responses. It allows one to be passionate without losing control. It remains calm.

• Is our religious or non-religious position freely chosen?

How central is my personal position for or against religion to my own life? Do I feel as if I can ask any questions and express my doubts about my own position without fear? This is true even if I am an atheist, agnostic, skeptic, or non-Christian.

Examining seriously and healing our own relationship to religion might be the most important step, and probably the hardest, to take. It's easier to move into anti-right-wing criticism and activism and thereby to not deal with our own issues about religion just as they refuse to do.

Activism too can function as an addiction. When it does, it's guaranteed to end in burnout, bitterness, and divisiveness.

(2) Dealing with the addiction requires clarity about why the addiction itself and the addict matter to us.

• Why are we in this fight?

Why do we care? Why have we been trying to change or control the addict?

This is not to say we should not respond or fight back. It's about clarity as to why this particular discussion or confrontation means something to our causes and us.

If the religiously addicted are our parents, why do we spend so much energy trying to change them? Are we still trying to get their love and approval? Why are we letting their ideas dominate our life? What keeps us from saying: "Dad. Mom. If you want to be around me, this is how you have to act."

If the addicted are our teenage or adult children, why do we continue to try to control them? Are we afraid of being misunderstood or perceived as inadequate parents? Do we need our children to turn out a certain way for us to feel good about ourselves? Are we afraid we'll lose their love, that they will abandon us?

If they are politicians, how do they control our lives? Why is our goal not just changing their legislative actions? Why do we also need their approval? Why will we not stand up for our beliefs because we are worried they will be offended when we stand up passionately for what we believe?

If it's members of the religious right, why do we protect them? Why, in the midst of all the ways they are promoting actions towards others and ourselves that are offensive, are we worried about offending their feelings? Do we *need* to save them?

• **There's no place for codependency.**

There's no place for the need to be liked or affirmed by the person with the addiction if we intend to stop enabling. AlAnon knows that. Yet the desire to be affirmed by religiously addicted parents, friends, children, ministers, leaders, and the enablers in the media, is classic codependency.

Melody Beattie in *Codependent No More* defined a codependent person as "one who has let another person's behavior affect him or her, and who is obsessed with controlling that person's behavior."

It's one thing to actually be dependent upon the addict in the manner that a small child or a teenager is dependent upon their parents for financial support. It's another thing for an adult to allow another adult's behavior to define their life for them even if that adult is their parent.

It's one thing if the addict is one's boss. Clarity means that I know I am not confronting the addiction in order to keep my job. That's a choice I can make and live with without guilt or shame. It's another thing to worry about how another adult with whom I have no financial or legal connection will think of me.

A relationship or non-relationship to a religious addict that is healthy for us requires clarity of purpose, freedom from the need to fix the addict, and doing what maintains one's own health and safety.

(3) Dealing with religious addiction requires recognizing the difference between addictive religion and non-addictive religion.

Some religion scholars see this difference in terms of theological ideas that are dangerous. Holding beliefs these researchers consider destructive, or propagating those beliefs as exclusive, absolute truths at the expense of most others, constitute for these analysts unhealthy religion.

In his *When Religion Becomes Evil,* Baptist religion professor Charles Kimball argues that there are five signs that warn us of the corruption of religion:

(1) When people make absolute truth claims, presuming to know God, abuse sacred texts, and propagate their particular view of absolute truth.

(2) When religion limits people's intellectual freedom and personal responsibility, making them dependent upon charismatic leaders or particular ideas.

(3) When religious leaders claim to establish an "ideal" time and believe they are agents of the Divine to establish the rule of the religious, a theocracy.

(4) When compassionate and constructive relationships with others are discarded to establish some idea, institution, or space considered sacred.

(5) When they declare holy war, justifying violence in the name of the Divine.

There are, as I have argued, certain beliefs that set the stage for addictive responses. Sociologists Christopher G.

Ellison and Darren E. Sherkat, for example, in "Obedience and Authority: Religion and Parental Values Reconsidered," argue that belief in Biblical literalism is correlated with the lack of valuation of intellectual autonomy in children and the resulting inability of abused children to even recognize that they were abused. Their conclusion is that ultra-conservative American Christians are less likely to be able even to consider alternative ideas to those of their addictive thinking. The past abuse prepared the human psyche for being comfortable with addictive religion.

My analysis instead emphasizes the place religion takes in someone's life more than what beliefs a believer holds. In fact, people on any place along the religious belief spectrum from the theological right to the theological left can use religion addictively.

Here I ask the question of how religion *functions* for people. How on the basis of a person's own stance toward their religion, its beliefs, practices, and institutions, can we identify a religious addict from someone who is not addicted?

• Do these religious people exhibit an attitude of relaxed learning toward their beliefs when others question them?

Remember Leo Booth's words in *When God Becomes a Drug*: "People who are spiritually healthy will not react with fear and anger to questions about their beliefs and practices."

When one discusses religion with non-addicted people, they're interested in listening and learning. They seek out information. They might not agree, but they are willing to read, listen, question, and explore ideas. They want to learn, to find out what they don't know. They're not threatened by disagreement and alternative viewpoints and, therefore, don't react defensively.

If you offer them a book that has helped you, they are sincerely interested. They don't immediately respond with defensive, closed tactics that protect them from what they perceive are threats to the truth of their beliefs or the perfection of the religious institutions they desperately cling to for relief.

In response to a book on theology or politics they don't fire back with: "That book's by a liberal. I'm not interested in what they have to say." In response to a book about the Bible, they don't retort: "I believe what the Bible says. I don't have to read someone's opinion about it." In response to a book on gay issues, they don't react: "Is that author gay? I don't read books that are biased."

These defensive responses may vary from a variety of verbal reactions to actions meant to destroy the threat. Obviously the Spanish Inquisition, Crusades and other religious wars, burning of witches, condemning of secular education, and demonizing people they turn into their enemies are defensive reactions of addictive religion. Such reactions function to protect the addictive thinking from all challenges that can be seen as terrifying threats to the supply chain of an addict's high.

In AA language, these reactions are those of addicts "protecting their stash." They're afraid. They don't want what they've become dependent upon taken away or questioned. Deception and violence can quickly characterize the response of addicts who are backed into a corner out of fear that they'll never get that fix again.

Addictions also win over relationships. The single-minded desire for the high of righteousness can ultimately make any activity that hurts those around the addict seem warranted.

With the addition of the idea that it's God's Truth, the destruction of others can also seem just, and even loving, to the religiously addicted. After all, they believe God does it.

• **Are the religious people open about being on their own journey?**

Twerski points out: "One of the features of addictive thinking is the addict's perception of always being right. Many of the other traits prevalent in addictive thinking — denial, projection, rationalization, omnipotence — are brought into play to bolster the insistence that the person has always been right." No wonder that the tenth step of AA advises: "And when wrong, promptly admit it."

Addictive religion doesn't directly proclaim that the people who believe it are perfect. Its doctrine of human evil enforces their imperfection.

Instead, it declares itself and, therefore, the beliefs that the religious person holds to be unquestionably right. It's their addiction that's perfect. On this matter, though a bit more subtle, the perfectionist function of the addictive thinking is still the same.

Addictive religion doesn't say: this is how I interpret or understand the Bible or God's will. It doesn't allow for further revelation or information. Its canon is closed or controlled by dogma and leaders.

Instead, addictive religion claims that it knows with certainty what God, or the Bible, says. There is no room for development or a change of understanding.

Not taking responsibility for their beliefs (as discussed in chapter four) means the addicted believer doesn't have to look deeply into herself or himself. They're protected from examining prejudices and personal issues that predispose the addicted believer to their addiction. They don't have to face the threat that their beliefs might be wrong, immature, or prejudiced.

Even though addictive religion has changed throughout history, it always must believe that its *current* understanding is unchangeable truth, unaffected by cultural influence. When it burned witches, crusaded in the Holy Land, claimed God supported slavery, or sanctioned wife-beating, it was certain then that those practices were the eternal will of God for all ages and cultures.

Today it might look back at those claims disapprovingly, but it has replaced them with ideas that they now claim to be similarly the real unchanging truth. Today, finally, in their new and improved righteousness, they believe, they aren't making those kinds of mistakes. "We've got it right now."

Non-addictive religious people know they're on a journey. This doesn't mean they are relativists who have no sense of absolute truths or right and wrong. But they are open to further information and change. They consider, discuss, learn, and make decisions about what is or is not acceptable.

Like a physician who gets new information from further diagnostic tests, when that new information arrives, they can actually change their mind. And they can do so without feeling that changing their mind means they are horrible, lost sinners.

They can ask for forgiveness if necessary for their previous beliefs and actions. They probably, in fact, believe that asking for forgiveness and personal repentance are central elements of their faith. As the ninth step of AA puts it, they can "make amends" to the people they have "harmed." They even consider this to be a key requirement for their own personal growth.

They take responsibility for their understanding of the Bible or God's will. They don't blame God or the Bible so as not to have to confront the personal and cultural prejudices that they might be using to understand them. They know that prejudice and cultural influences have affected past understandings and are likely to continue to affect them. Such an approach, however, threatens addictive religion and the high of righteousness.

Even more, non-addicted religious people are public about being on a journey. They're transparent about it. They're not frightened by the idea that they are people in process and that their faith is too. Though the addicted may criticize them for doing so, the non-addicted believe that a healthy life is necessarily a journey of exploration both internally and externally.

• Are they uninterested in, not obsessed with, condemning other people's journeys?

Judgmentalism is central to addictions. It accompanies a

rigidity of thought that sees no basis for other people's ideas except their evil nature or their sins.

Usually a result of insecurity about the truth of one's own beliefs, the compulsion to judge others becomes a using activity for the addict. Focusing on the wrongness of others keeps the insecurity about one's beliefs at bay. By spending time judging others, religious addicts reinforce their feeling that they are in the right.

It's no surprise, for example, when the most anti-gay right-wing minister or politician turns out to be gay themselves. Contemporary news is replete with the stories of conservative ministers and politicians who garnered much attention by working against the equal rights of gay people only to be found on the Internet or in a police sting soliciting gay sex.

Look too deeply into the histories of women who are outspoken in the movement to promote government limitation of women's reproductive rights and you find women who have not been able to forgive themselves for their past abortions. A large number of anti-choice activists have admitted to multiple abortions. Instead of facing and healing those emotions, anti-choice crusaders promote the very existence of guilt and shame and then provide activities to cope with those feelings through the high of righteousness.

News stories of the most publicly judgmental religious and political leaders who've suppressed their own practices of what they condemn are so common that one can hardly fault someone for suspecting that, as the first-century New Testament writer, Paul wrote to addicted believers: "wherein you judge another, you condemn yourself; for you who judge do the same things." Or, as Booth reminds religious addicts: "Projecting all of your self-hatred onto others, you judge them as harshly as you judge yourself — always pronouncing on others the same guilty verdict you secretly impose on yourself."

No matter whether or not the core problem behind such judgmentalism really is hypocritical participation in, or constant suppression of, one's own similar issues, the need to judge others is a telling factor that helps us recognize religious addiction. The question is: Why *must* they do this? What's the real compulsion behind judging others? Answering, "God tells me to do so" is to blame God or the Bible again for an obsessive need to stay high on righteousness.

It goes deeper than whether or not a religious addict publicly judges others, including other religious people, who don't agree with them. Many of the leaders of addictive religion are openly judgmental of believers in their very own traditions, accusing them of heresy and declaring that those who disagree with them and still claim to be of their brand of Christianity are the cause of their own religion's demise.

Non-addicted religious people hold their beliefs but not at the expense of others. As one theologian understood Christianity: "A Christian is someone who has been freed from the need to judge others."

Without the need to do so, non-addicted religious people have no interest in judging others and don't understand why other people would do so either. It's just not a part of their lifestyle.

• **Are they not limited by either/or, for us/against us, thinking?**

Either/or, good or evil, black or white thinking without nuance and subtlety is a mark of addictions including addictive religion. The mental incapacity to see that moral decisions often call for choosing the lesser of evils or the better of goods results in polarizing discussions of religious, ethical, and social issues by the addicted. One gets the impression that they can't think otherwise.

This either/or thinking also results in us/them thinking. One must either fully embrace the addictive religion, even its clichés, practices, and doctrinal details, or one is an enemy. Even other Christians become enemies as "heretics, enemies of the gospel, or relativists." For many addicted people it's almost worse to say you're a Christian but disagree than be a full-fledged atheist.

It's even worse if you are open about your disagreements with them. They'd prefer that nothing those who disagree with them do meet them face to face. Liberals in the closet are okay. They should neither be seen nor heard.

Remember, framing theological and ethical ideas and actions in terms of either/or is a means of controlling life. It requires reducing difficult situations to neat and tidy solutions that are abstractly above the human beings with the problems. It provides a feeling of certainty in an uncertain world that threatens the addict. And the mainstream media has come to love it.

(4) Be clear about what you can and cannot do for the addict and the addiction.

It's not surprising that recovery groups often use the old "Serenity Prayer" credited to twentieth-century Lutheran theologian Reinhold Niebuhr: "God grant me the serenity to accept the things I cannot change; courage to change the things I can; and wisdom to know the difference."

Whether or not we believe in prayer, there's practical wisdom in the idea of knowing what can be done and not focusing on what's out of our control. Since we didn't cause religious addiction and can't control or cure it, we can only do things that advance our own healthy lives and prevent the results of the addiction from affecting the rest of us.

With addicts in place in high and powerful places in our society and religious addiction enabled by many of our institutions, we begin with the question: Do we have a positive enough self-image to refuse to be abused by those who won't face the addiction? This question also includes so-called liberal politicians who treat many of their constituents as those rich, eccentric relatives whom they come to for support but try to hide out of sight when people ask them who those relatives over there are?

Are we willing to face the fact that we'll still be affected by the addiction and, therefore, that we have to live our lives in the light of that fact to protect ourselves and our safety? Since addicts do hit bottom, are we certain that we won't be under the addicts, trying to prop them up, when they do fall? Are we actively working to become independent of the addict?

Are we able to say that they, not we, are the problem? Are we no longer making excuses for the addict? Have we stopped covering up for the addict? Are we setting the agenda or are we letting the addict be the center of attention even when *we* respond to *their agenda* negatively?

(5) Remove the addict and the addiction from the driver's seat in our society and lives, through non-codependent, non-coaddictive, strategies.

• **Stop trying to figure out the addict and the addiction** as if figuring them out would change it. It won't, as AlAnon and addition specialists know.

Remember Twerski's emphatic advice: "I cannot stress enough the importance of realizing that addicts are taken in by their distorted thinking and that they are its victims. If we fail to understand this, we may feel frustrated or angry in dealing with the addict."

Liberal people are convinced that if they understand a person and their thinking they'll be able to help the person or learn how better to respond to change the person. When more understanding doesn't work, though, they assume that even more of their energy should be wasted trying to understand how the addict's mind works. This unending search for "understanding" is another way liberals blame themselves for the continuance of the addiction.

It's just not true that the problem with addictions is that those outside the addiction can't figure out the thinking of the addict. There is therefore no need to try to understand the logic of the addict or the addict's thinking in order to make progress.

Trying to understand their "real" motives, intentions, or personal histories is guaranteed to drive people who feel they

ىٮ to figure it out crazy. It's a waste of time and a distraction ırom our own process of dealing in a healthy manner with the addict.

Codependent people spend considerable time and emotional energy looking for the key to understanding addicts. It can be come obsessive.

Trying to find the logic in the addiction only accomplishes three unhealthy things:

(1) It focuses on the addict, allowing the addict to continue to be the center of attention.

(2) It prevents the codependent person from doing what it takes to separate emotionally from the addict and from breaking through their own reasons for being codependent in the first place.

(3) It keeps the codependent person from focusing on strategies that can actually change how the addict's behavior affects them.

• **Don't argue with an addict.**

Arguing with an addict is playing the addict's game. It focuses attention away from the addicts' real issues and allows them to deny those real issues.

It makes something else — religion, the Bible, tradition, the media, or God — the center of attention, not the addict's real personal problems. It takes away addicts' need to accept responsibility for their actions, beliefs, and words.

That's why addicts prefer that the discussion be in their arena of abstraction that doesn't challenge their addictive thinking, while blaming others. It must never be about them personally.

Addictive religion does not want the discussion personalized for the believer as an individual. It has a difficult enough problem when people try to personalize the enemies it would rather speak of in abstract generalizations.

The change that must take place to leave an addiction is

that addicts must confront their own emotional issues and resulting prejudices, the issues that the addiction covers for them personally. Few people would prefer to delve into those emotionally charged issues rather than get into a discussion that isn't threatening to them. Even enabling is a way not to confront the personal issues of the enabler.

Arguing about God, the Bible, or tradition is like arguing with the alcoholic about whether whiskey or tequila is better for them. It's useless and affirms the addiction.

There are many interpretations of God and the passages of the Bible. Addicted people think their interpretation isn't merely one of many. It's the unbiased truth. Arguing which is better with a religious addict is useless.

History is full of ideas, activities, and events. "Tradition," often used as an argument, only means choosing what one wants to affirm from all of history and ignoring everything else.

Cockroaches are traditional. They've been around since the dinosaurs. They've been in most traditional families. Yet, one hears few "traditional family values" people arguing for their protection.

- **Don't let the addict get you off topic.**

Addicts love to confuse the issues, get you talking about things that don't challenge their problem. When you do, you further the addiction.

Never argue about whether sexual orientation is a choice. It doesn't matter.

Never argue about sex. Our country is too sick to deal with its sexual problems. If you're arguing about sexual education, stick with the need for education.

Never argue about whether those Founding Fathers agreed with you. They were rich, white males who decided that people of color were only worth one-fifth of a white person. For all the good they did to get the US started, they were hardly perfect models of moral values and religious beliefs.

Stay on task. If you're seeking safe schools for all children, keep that the center of your discussion. If you want the government not to control women's bodies, say so again and again. If you believe the government has no right to tell two consenting adults whom they can and cannot love, don't get caught in side discussions. If you seek equal opportunity for all people regardless of race or ethnicity, keep that the center of your message as if that really is the important issue to you. If poison-free neighborhoods are your cause, keep the message on pollution hurting people.

• **Don't nag addicts.**

Constantly nagging addicts also keeps the addiction at the center of your attention. The goal of nagging is to change the addict rather than changing the dynamics of your life and society to make it better for you. It gives the addict all the power instead of focusing on where you can change things.

Don't speak belligerently or as if you have to defend yourself. No matter how maddening the language and immobility of the religious addict, belligerence and defensiveness rise out of insecurity in one's own position. They communicate that insecurity.

Addictive religion is based upon feelings of insecurity and fear of unbelief. Recognize that and model self-assurance.

• **Don't buy into the addict's view of reality.**

Addicts cover their addiction with a mythology about the world and with language that mystifies. In the recovery world it's called "stinkin' thinkin." Its goal is to maintain and promote the addiction.

The addictive mythology is a way of seeing the world that addicts would love the non-addicted to accept. Repeating their language or accepting their view of reality normalizes the addiction. It affirms in the addicts' minds their view of themselves and the world.

Addictive religion attempts to set the worldview of the country with its own ideas of the Bible, hell, Christ, the Divine, and good and evil. Many of the political initiatives of addictive religion are meant to mainstream their worldview for the next generation they still fear they're losing.

This means don't affirm their view of reality by using the language of addiction. Language repeated enforces the view of reality of the addiction in the minds of the media and others.

Never say, even to reject it or with "so-called" before it: "partial-birth abortion," "gay rights," "intelligent design," "gay marriage," "the government," etc. Speak clearly in terms of what you believe it really is. Say "a seldom used late-term procedure," "equal rights for all," "government interference in women's bodies," "creationist ideology," "marriage equality," "the administration."

Learn about framing and re-framing the debate from linguists such as George Lakoff. Remember, though, that this doesn't merely mean changing the language we use. It means speaking out of non-addictive values, using language that communicates those values you believe in, and doing so over the long haul.

• **Don't accept the idea that the addiction needs equal time.**

Get over any guilt about a free country requiring you to make more space for addictive arguments. Addicts and their dealers already have the power of the addiction and addictive communities behind their messages.

They have their own media. They have the enabling presence of a mainstream media that has come to think that identifying only two sides on an issue is enough and that both sides have equal validity. In a culture where addictive thinking is dominant and commercially exploitable, this approach promotes addictions.

You don't have to act as if there are "two sides" to every debate. Stop debating as if there are two equal sides. "Fair and balanced" is an idea meant to portray all issues as having two equally worthy sides no matter how unsupported one of them is by evidence.

Though liberal people feel as if they must say, "I respect your position," stop and think before you do. You can respect people but not necessarily a destructive position they take on an issue. If you believe that the opposite position of your own is equally true and respectable, ask yourself why you care to disagree with it at all. Just for sport?

• **Get your message on target and be willing to repeat it and repeat it.**

Get support for your message from others so that they're on the same page. Make it short, simple, to the point, personal, and consistent.

Educators know the value of repetition. Repeating a point means you think it's worth repeating. It also emphasizes that you believe it's important. The right-wing understands this.

Telling your own stories, giving your views, isn't arguable if these really are your stories and views. You don't have to be an expert to hold your views. If you know the statistics or the variety of Biblical interpretations of many passages that do exist, fine. However, people don't need statistics as much as they need to meet non-addictive people who are secure in their convictions without the addiction.

• **Take responsibility for what you believe to be true and right.**

Addicted people need to see that there are people who are willing to disagree with them. They need to meet these people in the flesh to be clear that they are out there.

The moveable middle of society is looking for the leadership of non-addicted people. They need healthy people to be public about their beliefs, values, and causes.

Don't blame God, the Bible, or tradition for your beliefs and stands. Use language such as: "I believe," "I understand," "No, I disagree," "I know a lot of people agree with you, but I don't."

Act as if you believe it with all your heart. Act as if your values aren't negotiable.

Do you really believe discrimination is wrong? Do you believe people should always be treated as valuable human beings? Do you believe the government has no right to tell women they either must or must not have an abortion? If so, how can you act as if these ideas are negotiable?

Even if addictive religion is supported by the powerful, Alice Miller reminds us: "In order to tell the truth we do not need to have power over others. Power is something we only need in order to spread lies and hypocrisy, to mouth empty words and pretend they are true."

Addicts argue as if people need addictive religion's beliefs to have morality, a civilized society, and healthy relationships. One can spend time arguing that this isn't true, but the convincing proof of its falsehood to most people is the visibility of people who speak of and act out of their healthy values without religious addiction.

• **Don't do it alone.**

The majority of people are not religiously addicted but feel as if there are no alternatives available to them. They don't see them in the mainstream media. In fact, the mainstream media often portray those outside society's accepted addictions as unappealing, counter-cultural (They are.), isolated, and weird. So, the majority of people who know something is wrong feel as if they'll be alone when they stop enabling the addiction.

Addicts reinforce each other. Fundamentalist religious organizations and media are their supportive co-users.

So the person who deals with someone's addiction cannot do it alone. They must have support from others outside the addiction. Find or create communities of support.

• **Model what it is to be a healthy human being without the addiction.**

Model healthy religion and moral values. Do this first for

yourself, your integrity, and your sense of justice and compassion.

Addictive religion tries to portray anyone who isn't caught up in the addiction as someone who lacks values, direction, and goals. It's the most likely to argue that atheists, agnostics, and other non-religious people have no moral standards. It argues that liberal Christians (along with liberal politicians) are all relativists without a moral compass.

It would love to picture all those outside the addiction the way it pictured the Skid Row bums that used to populate their stories of being saved. It wants those who disagree with them to appear troubled, and hates any visible pride these people have in their "alternative" beliefs and lifestyles.

Keeping any progressive lifestyles out of mainstream visibility or portraying them as the quaint minority lives of left-wing extremists prevents people from seeing successful alternatives. It prevents alternatives to their addiction from looking appealing. That's why progressives must come out of their various closets as progressives.

Addicts and those enabling them need to see people living outside the addiction, happy, confident, proud, and free from the effects of the disease. It must seem possible to contradict the teaching of addictive religion and live better for it.

In spite of the fact that we're a nation that supports both substance and process addictions so people don't threaten the institutions and values that pursue profits over humanity, the non-addicted must live as if that fact has no ultimate control over them.

- **Be gentle with yourself.**

This is most important. Give yourself a break.

Don't add to the guilt. You are not responsible for how others respond. You are responsible for your own health, security, and safety. You don't have to to this perfectly.

Give yourself permission not to engage, even to walk away.

You don't always have to be in "the fight." You only have to concern yourself with always maintaining your integrity.

Don't believe that you, your friends, children, relationships, hopes, and dreams, are any less valuable or legitimate because they aren't sanctioned by a government, politicians, or religious leaders that are in a coping, rather than healing, mode of life.

It's okay to affirm that you don't care about an encounter you have or that these aren't the issues. You don't need to justify your beliefs to a drunk or druggy.

THE BALL REALLY IS IN OUR COURT

Now, it's going to take awhile for addictive religion to hit bottom. It's on a new drug and it has mainstream approval. Short-term measures with immediate wins are not enough.

But does the addiction have our support? Are we the enablers?

Are we emotionally unable or unwilling to speak truth to the addict, saying the addiction is wrong, sick, and destructive? Are we unable to separate from the addiction? Are we unwilling to join the equivalent of support groups like ReligionAnon, or form Mothers Against Abusive Religion?

Once we've named an addiction, it's our choice how we live with an addict. It's our choice about whether we seek an addict's love and support. And it's our choice, knowing that addictions are hard to overcome, whether we're in it for the long haul because, in the end, we want to stop addictions from hurting everyone.

Dealing with addictions takes an emotional toll on everyone. Yet, recognizing religious addiction as an addiction demystifies its dynamics, maintains our sanity, provides hope for our communities and nation, and allows the non-addicted to act in ways that are more effective than those that enable the people for whom religion is an addiction.

Further Reading

Leo Booth. *When God Becomes a Drug: Breaking the Chains of Religious Addiction and Abuse*. New York: Tarcher/Putnam, 1991.

David Brock. *The Republican Noise Machine: Right-Wing Media and How It Corrupts Democracy*. New York: Crown, 2004.

Donald Capps. *The Child's Song: The Religious Abuse of Children*. Louisville: Westminster John Knox, 1995.

Patrick Carnes. *Out of the Shadows: Understanding Sexual Addiction*. 3rd ed. Center City: Hazelden, 2001.

Patrick Carnes. *Sexual Anorexia: Overcoming Sexual Self-Hatred*. Center City: Hazelden, 1997.

John W. Dean. *Conservatives Without Conscience*. New York: Viking, 2006.

Christopher G. Ellison and Darren E. Sherkat. "Obedience and Authority: Religion and Parental Values Reconsidered." *Journal for the Scientific Study or Religion* 32 (1993), 313-329.

Thomas Frank. *What's the Matter with Kansas: How Conservatives Won the Heart of America*. New York: Metropolitan Books, 2004.

Phillip Greven. *Spare the Child: The Religious Roots of Punishment and the Psychological Impact of Physical Abuse*. New York: Alfred Knopf, 1991.

Elizabeth Connell Henderson. *Understanding Addiction*. Jackson: University of Mississippi Press, 2000.

Charles Kimball. *When Religion Becomes Evil*. New York: HarperSan Francisco, 2002.

David Kuo, *Tempting Faith: An Inside Story of Political Seduction*. New York: Free Press, 2006.

George Lakoff. *Don't Think of an Elephant: Know Your*

Values and Frame the Debate. White River Junction: Chelsea Green, 2004.

George Lakoff. *Moral Politics: How Liberals and Conservatives Think.* 2nd ed. Chicago: University of Chicago Press, 2002.

Alice Miller. T*he Truth Will Set You Free: Overcoming Emotional Blindness and Finding Your True Adult Self.* New York: Basic Books, 2001.

Alice Miller. *For Your Own Good: Hidden Cruelty in Child-Rearing and the Roots of Violence.* New York: The Noonday Press, 1990.

Robert N. Minor. *Scared Straight: Why It's So Hard to Accept Gay People and Why It's So Hard to Be Human.* St. Louis: HumanityWorks!, 2001.

Elaine Pagels. *Adam, Eve and the Serpent.* New York: Vintage Books, 1988.

Bill Press. *How the Republicans Stole Christmas: The Republican Party's Declared Monopoly on Religion and What Democrats Can Do to Take It Back.* New York: Doubleday, 2005.

Uta Ranke-Heinemann. *Eunuchs for the Kingdom of Heaven: Women, Sexuality and the Catholic Church.* New York: Penguin Books, 1991.

Anne Wilson Schaef. *The Addictive Organization: Why We Overwork, Cover Up, Pick Up the Pieces, Please the Boss and Perpetuate Sick Organizations.* New York: HarperSan Francisco, 1988.

Anne Wilson Schaef. *Escape from Intimacy: Untangling the "Love" Addictions: Sex, Romance, Relationships.* New York: HarperSan Francisco, 1989.

Anne Wilson Schaef. *When Society Becomes an Addict.* New York: HarperSan Francisco, 1987.

Hal Taussig. *A New Spiritual Home: Progressive Christianity at the Grass Roots.* Santa Rosa: Polebridge Press, 2006.

Leonore Tiefer. *Sex Is Not a Natural Act.* 2nd ed. Boulder: Westview Press, 2004.

Abraham J. Twerski. *Addictive Thinking: Understanding Self-Deception.* 2nd ed. Center City: Hazelden, 1997.

Mel White. *Religion Gone Bad: The Hidden Dangers of the Christian Right.* New York: Jeremy P. Tarcher/Penguin, 2006.

ABOUT THE AUTHOR

Robert N. Minor received his Masters of Arts degree in Biblical Studies from Trinity Divinity School and his Ph.D. in Religion from the University of Iowa. He is currently Professor of Religious Studies at the University of Kansas where he has taught since 1977 and was department chair for six years. *When Religion Is an Addiction* is his eighth book. He has written on religion in India as well as religion and sexuality and gender. He is a popular writer, speaker and workshop leader nationally and founder of The Fairness Project. He lives in Kansas City, Missouri.

ACKNOWLEDGEMENTS

There are many books about finding Mr. or Ms. Right, keeping Mr. or Ms. Right, and recovering after losing Mr. or Ms. Right only to search again. There are few books, if any, about how to be a better friend to someone. I have been fortunate enough that the people I want to thank for their other roles have also shown me by their constant support what good friends are — Brenda Bobo-Fisher and Mahrya Monson of HumanityWorks!, the pioneering men of the Lawrence Men's Group, Professor Robert D. Baird and Professors Sandra and Paul Zimdars-Swartz, my brother, sisters and mom and dad, my son Matt, Jamie Rich of Open Circle, Paul Haughey of Quest Living, Rev. Martin Rafanan of the National Conference for Community and Justice of Metropolitan St. Louis, Rev. Thad Holcomb of Ecumenical Christian Ministries at the University of Kansas, Rev. Paul Smith and Rev. Marsha Fleishman and the members of Broadway Church, and Gary Rockhold.

ALSO BY ROBERT N. MINOR

SCARED STRAIGHT: WHY IT'S SO HARD TO ACCEPT GAY PEOPLE AND WHY IT'S SO HARD TO BE HUMAN

Why is our country still stuck on the issue of accepting gay people fully? There's something deeper going on. From the criticism of our universities as purveyors of hopelessness to the dynamics of "Getting Laid," Robert Minor creates a penetrating analysis of U.S. culture. A finalist for both the Lambda Literary Award and the Independent Publishers Book Award, *Scared Straight* gets to the heart of the matter.

ISBN: 0-9709581-0-2

GAY & HEALTHY IN A SICK SOCIETY: THE MINOR DETAILS

A finalist for the Independent Publishers Book Award and recommended by MenStuff.org, the nation's premier men's resource website, *Gay & Healthy* discusses sex, gender, leadership, politics, relationships, and society. Robert Minor argues in this inspirational collection that in our critically ill culture, those who refuse to act "straight," no matter what sexual orientation, can live healthier lives, develop relationships they really want, and be a voice for healing society.

ISBN: 0-9709581-1-0

HumanityWorks!
A CONSORTIUM BUILDING:

Available at your favorite bookseller
or online at www.FairnessProject.org